ABORIGINES AND THE 'SPORT OF KINGS'

INDIGENOUS JOCKEYS IN AUSTRALIAN RACING HISTORY

Revised Edition

JOHN MAYNARD

Aboriginal Studies Press

First published in 2002 by Aboriginal Studies Press [or the Australian Institute of Aboriginal and Torres Strait Islander Studies, GPO *Box 553*. Canberra ACT 2601.

© First edition John Maynard 2002
© Second edition John Maynard 2003
© Third edition John Maynard 2013

All rights reserved. No part of this book may be reproduced or transmitted in any form or by any means, electronic or mechanical, including photocopying, recording or by any information storage and retrieval system, without prior permission in writing from the publisher. The *Australian Copyright Act 1968* (the Act) allows a maximum of one chapter or 10 per cent of this book, whichever is the greater, to be photocopied by any educational institution for its education purposes provided that the educational institution (or body that administers it) has given a remuneration notice to Copyright Agency Limited (CAL) under the Act.

National Library of Australia cataloguing-in-publication data:

Author: Maynard, John, 1954- author.

Title: *Aborigines and the 'sport of kings'*/John Maynard.

Edition: 3rd edition.

ISBN: 9781922059543 (paperback)
ISBN: 9781922059444 (ebook: pdf)

Notes: Includes bibliographical references and index. Previous edition: *Aboriginal stars of the turf: jockeys of Australian racing history*/John Maynard, 2002.

Subjects: Jockeys — Australia — Biography. Racehorse trainers — Australia — Biography. Aboriginal Australian jockeys — Biography. Horse racing —Australia — History.

Dewey Number: 798.4009239915

Text design and typesetting by Greg Jorrs, Upside Creative

Front cover: Lyall Appo winning the Mansell Concrete 1200mm on *Youthful*, 2002. Photograph by Barry Pascoe, courtesy Newspix.

The publisher has made every effort to contact copyright owners for permission to use material reproduced in this book. The publisher would be pleased to hear from copyright holders of any errors or omissions.

DEDICATION

To the hundreds of Aboriginal jockeys who have followed their dreams to the racecourse.

In particular, it is dedicated to Leigh-Anne Goodwin — Australia's first female Aboriginal jockey to ride a winner at a metropolitan track. Leigh-Anne died on 7 December 1998 in Brisbane hospital after a fall at Roma.

This book is a testament to their skills, their records and victories, and to their conquering of prejudice and racism.

FOREWORD

It is a great pleasure to write a foreword for this important study of Aboriginal jockeys and their contribution to the history of horseracing in Australia. Until the last twenty or thirty years historians simply ignored, and by implication denied, the roles played by Aborigines in a whole range of popular sports and pastimes. This applied in particular to histories of horseracing. As recently as 1987 Neville Penton's *A racing heart: The story of the Australian turf* simply referred to Rae (Togo) Johnstone as 'swarthy', while his account of Darby McCarthy's turf exploits made no reference to his Indigenous origins. Similarly, Jack Pollard's, encyclopaedia of Australian horseracing, which was first published in 1988 and is regarded as something of a bible by turf historians, contains only a brief and inadequate entry on Aboriginal jockeys. Pollard, at least acknowledges that Darby McCarthy was an Aborigine. Pollard once interviewed Rae Johnstone at a time when the latter was a highly successful rider based in France. Noting that Johnstone showed little interest in visiting his hometown of Sydney Pollard was puzzled and noted, 'It was though there was something there that he wanted to forget.' It didn't occur to Pollard that Johnstone didn't wish to compromise his social status in Europe. After all, in the post Second World War era racism was not a uniquely Australian phenomenon. I regret to add that the official history of the Australian Jockey Club (AJC), which I co-authored and which was published in 1992 to mark the sesquicentenary of the club's founding, also neglected the role of Aboriginal jockeys in the history of racing at Randwick and Warwick Farm. So, what makes John Maynard's book important is that it is the first comprehensive account of the significant contribution of Aboriginal jockeys to an institution which is not only a major Australian sport, but also a highly influential Australian cultural institution.

Academic historians of Australian society, culture and even sport have tended to ignore horse racing. Beginning with Frank Wilkinson's unpublished history of the AJC, most histories of horseracing were and are written by insiders or journalists. The lack of attention from professional historians is in fact quite odd because from its establishment in the late eighteenth andearly nineteenth centuries until about the end of the Second World War it stood, along with theatre, as one of the two most popular and influential cultural institutions in Australia. Writing in the late nineteenth century EC Buley noted that the first concern of settlers setting up a new town was to establish a cemetery and the second was to lay out a racecourse. It is true that for the first ninety years or so of its existence Sydney featured less than twenty race meetings a year but with the establishment of pony and proprietary racing in the 1880s that number grew to in excess of one hundred and thirty — on average more than two meetings a week. Racing began to lose its central cultural role after the Second World War, and although it was given a temporary stimulus with the establishment of TABs in the 1960s (resulting in a much needed influx of funds into the industry) the emergence of new forms of entertainment and the establishment of alternative forms of gambling, meant that racing declined in status and influence.

As noted, there is a long-standing tendency among historians to ignore or downplay the contribution of Aborigines to the creation and development of a whole range of local cultural institutions. Only in recent times have historians begun to explore the roles of Indigenous people in games like cricket, pedestrianism, boxing, Australian Rules, Rugby League, football (soccer) and, of course, horseracing. It is the outstanding achievement of this book that using rigorous research methods John Maynard has brought to light the major role of Aboriginal jockeys in one of Australia's most important cultural institutions.

This book is not just scholarly; it is also highly informative and accessible. What makes John Maynard particularly well qualified to tell this story is that he is unique among racing historians because while he possesses academic qualifications he is also an insider who grew up in the industry as the son of the renowned jockey Merv Maynard. And what emerges from his biographies is a larger story about the experience of Aborigines in the racing industry. Like their European counterparts, Aboriginal jockeys faced danger every time they rode, and some like Merv Marion and Leigh-Anne Goodwin suffered severe injuries from race falls, which in the case of Goodwin resulted in her tragic death. Racing is notorious as a sport of fickle fortune and some of Maynard's case studies demonstrate how some Aboriginal jockeys accumulated considerable wealth, although a few of them, and Darby McCarthy is an outstanding example, promptly lost almost everything they had accumulated. Their careers were sometimes not so different from the most successful jockeys of European descent. Rae (Togo) Johnstone enjoyed fabulous success riding for the most famous trainers and wealthiest owners in Europe. It was a career that closely mirrored Edgar Britt's. But the hurdles facing Aboriginal jockeys were far higher because they endured what their European counterparts did not — racial prejudice. And they adopted a number of strategies to cope with this situation. Some, like Rae (Togo) Johnstone, denied they were Aborigines. Others, like Massa Reid refused to ride in places like Sydney where they expected to find a greater degree of prejudice than in the towns in which they rode and were known. Others, and Darby McCarthy is a shining example, not only embraced their Aboriginal backgrounds but sought to open more opportunities in racing for the young Aboriginal riders who followed them into the industry.

Australia has two histories, one that belongs to European Australians and the other which belongs to the original Indigenous inhabitants of this land. But from 1788 those histories also became intertwined as Aboriginal people learnt to adapt to European society, even as they continued to resist it. They excelled as shepherds, shearers (when permitted), stockriders, and entertainers (especially as circus performers). They also proved to be outstanding jockeys, something that sporting journalists as well as cultural historians seem to have forgotten. This outstanding book is a case study in survival and achievement in the face of adversity.

Richard Waterhouse
University of Sydney

CONTENTS

Foreword by Richard Waterhouse - - - - - - - - - - - - - - - - - - iv
Preface - viii
Acknowledgements - xi
Introduction: Aboriginal jockeys —
a proud past but an uncertain future? - - - - - - - - - - - - - - - 1

PART I: BEHIND THE BARRIERS — THE BACKGROUND TO INDIGENOUS INVOLVEMENT IN RACING

The Arrival of the horse - 8
Off and Racing: Characters and yarns from the Inner Sanctum - - - 11
Identity, Racing and Racism - - - - - - - - - - - - - - - - - - - 17
Aboriginal Women in Racing - - - - - - - - - - - - - - - - - - - 23
To the Finish Line - 26

PART II: RIDING HIGH: THE STARS OF THE TURF

Peter St Albans - 31
Rae 'Togo' Johnstone - 49
David Hugh 'Darby' Munro - 60
Merv Maynard - 65
Frank Reys - 81
Norm Rose - 87
Richard Lawrence 'Darby' McCarthy - - - - - - - - - - - - - - - 94
Leigh-Anne Goodwin - 105

PART III: AHEAD OF THE FIELD: MORE INDIGENOUS AUSTRALIAN JOCKEYS

Charlie Flannigan - 110
Percy Kennedy - 111
Massa Read - 112
Jimmy Dries - 112
Besley Murray - 113

Stan Johnson - 115
Kenny Broderick - 116
Barry Hagan - 117
Frank and Jack Duval - - - - - - - - - - - - - - - - - 117
Doug Hodgson - 119
Gordon Taylor - 122
Jimmy Leslie - 123
Harry Fuller - 123
Bill O'Brien - 123
David Mathews - 124
Merv Marion - 127
Reg 'Punter' Hart - 127
William Lord - 129
Geoff Booth - 129
Glen Pickwick - 130
Lyall Appo - 132
Bradley Appo - 140
Paul Timbery - 141
Rosalyn and Rod Bynder - - - - - - - - - - - - - - 142
Gaynor Chambers - - - - - - - - - - - - - - - - - - - 146

Bibliography - 147
Index - 150

PREFACE

When I first wrote *Aboriginal Stars of the Turf* back in 2002, it was about exposing the myth of limited Aboriginal involvement in Australian horse racing and why Aboriginal jockeys were not recognised. The Aboriginal riders in this book are just a few of the many great Aboriginal jockeys who have ridden through Australia's racing history.

I wish to acknowledge all the Aboriginal jockeys — men and women — who have graced Australian racecourses over the past two hundred years but who do not appear here. As time goes by and my own knowledge and information are enhanced, I hope to recognise many more of these deserving people.

At the heart of this study was a passion and desire to play some small part in the process of revealing another important missing chapter of Australian Aboriginal history. For nearly two centuries, our stories have been derided, hidden and even erased. Yet the mists of the past continue to lift and reveal rich tales of survival and inspiration. We are only now at the very beginning of this process, and our stories can and will play an important role in recognising that over the past two centuries and more, the historical tapestry of this country has been one in which both black and white have been deeply interwoven.

Today, more than a decade after the book first appeared, Aboriginal involvement in Australian racing appears not to be at the same levels as it was in the past. Why have Aboriginal youth looked towards other sporting and employment opportunities? This revised edition will explore these changes and also examine riders who were missed in the past and those who have broken through since 2003.

I think it is important to note that my credentials to write this book come from the fact that I was born at the track. My knowledge of racing was not learnt from reading books or studying racing. Our family stories tell that by the time I was 12 months old I had been in every town in New South Wales — or at least those with a racetrack (and there are not too many towns without one). When I was 4, we lived in New Zealand for a year as my father was riding there; at 8 we were in Singapore and Malaysia, as he had a riding contract for four years in Asia.

Our family — particularly on my maternal line — is steeped in racing tradition: two of my maternal grandmother's brothers were jockeys, her son Eric Middleton was a jockey and later trainer, her son-in-law (my father) was a jockey, and her other son-in-law Ray Wallace was a great money trainer with top class metropolitan winners like Peninsula, Bungan Head and Calico Chief. My maternal grandfather had two cousins who were at the very top of any jockeys' list: Harold Badger and

THE AUTHOR AGED THREE DISPLAYING A NEAT SEAT IN THE SADDLE. COURTESY MAYNARD FAMILY COLLECTION.

the legendary Jim Pike, rider of Phar Lap. My grandmother's brother, Wallace, was killed at Caulfield going over the steeple jumps on Caulfield Cup Day in 1926.

I was riding before I could walk, but a few busters off the family pony and the fact that I was never going to carry a jockey weight convinced me to pursue another career direction. As a young teenager, I recall my father saying to me, 'Son, if you want to be a jockey, you'd better go to India and ride elephants.' Over the years, I maintained an interest in racing, and during the 1970s and 1980s I was fortunate to travel the globe on International Racehorse Transport (IRT), caring for globe-trotting thoroughbreds. At one point, I was a horse float driver and transported some top gallopers — including dual Newmarket winner Razor Sharp.

During that period, I used to swim horses three mornings a week in Newcastle Harbour off Horseshoe Beach. One funny incident I recall was trying to get a horse into the water for Newcastle trainer and character Bill Vallis. The horse had the nickname of Lurch because he was so slow moving and would just dig his feet in like a mule. There we were at the water's edge when Bill said, 'I'll leg you up and you can ride him in.' I was sitting on Lurch's back trying to coax him into

PREFACE

THE AUTHOR RECEIVES AN EARLY RIDING LESSON FROM HIS FATHER MERV MAYNARD. COURTESY MAYNARD FAMILY COLLECTION.

the water, then happened to glance over my back just in time to see Bill bring down a big piece of driftwood on Lurch's rump! Lurch and I must have resembled a Cape Kennedy rocket heading skywards. We plunged into the water about 15 metres from shore before coming back up, and Lurch was swimming like an equine Mark Spitz!

There were so many characters at the track during my young life — real horsemen and women. Sadly, they are nearly all gone today. My desire to write the stories of Aboriginal jockeys was, of course, driven by the fact that, having been brought up on the track, I was well aware that Aboriginal jockeys were rarely mentioned in Australian racing histories. I grew up knowing a whole host of them: Stan Johnson, Gordon Taylor, Normie Rose and Darby McCarthy were all riding at the same time as my father. I used to have a picture of Darby McCarthy that I cut out of either the *Telegraph* or *Mirror*, arriving at Ascot in top hat and tails from a Rolls Royce. It was such an inspiring image.

This book is my way of ensuring that Aboriginal riders are afforded their just place in Australian racing history.

John Maynard, 2013

ACKNOWLEDGEMENTS

I wish to thank the following individuals and agencies for their support and permission to reproduce images for which they hold copyright: Bradley Photographers; Douglass Baglin; Eileen Rallah and Michael Aird; Newspix/News Limited; the Australian Racing Museum; the *Centralian Advocate*; The *Courier-Mail*; the Mitchell Library, State Library of New South Wales; the National Library of Australia; the *Newcastle Herald*; the *NT News*; the Richard Buchhorn collection; the *Sun-Herald*; *Turf Monthly*; and Wendy McWhinney and the Geelong Gallery.

I also wish to thank all the families of the jockeys and other individuals who have provided information or images, particularly Bill Lord, Bill Thorpe, Colin Tatz, Don Elphick, Kenny Broderick's family, the Maynard family, the Duval family, the Hodgson family and Besley Murray.

I am grateful to all the family members and community groups who lent time and support throughout my research project, culminating in this second revision of *Aboriginal Stars of the Turf*. I value the fact that you recognised the importance of this project and put your faith in me. All of you have helped me to realise the goal of revealing these missing chapters of our history.

The racing fraternity has also responded well, including the Australian Jockey Club (AJC), the Victorian Racing Club (VRC), the South Australian Jockey Club (SAJC) and the Newcastle Jockey Club (NJC).

I would have found it virtually impossible without the backing and support of my colleagues at Wollotuka and Umulliko at the University of Newcastle. The first article I wrote and had published on this topic appeared in the *Aboriginal History* journal, and I acknowledge the support of the board of *Aboriginal History* and the Stanner Award during that period. The support of Dr Peter Read and Dr Geoff Gray has been ongoing since that time.

A research grant from the Australian Institute of Aboriginal and Torres Strait Islander Studies (AIATSIS) helped me develop the original manuscript for *Aboriginal Stars of the Turf*. The Institute's publishing arm, Aboriginal Studies Press, has lent wonderful support and guidance, and has been passionately committed to the publishing of my book. I thank the publishing team of Kelly, Jo-anne, Ros, Rachel, Tony and Sandra (2002) and the current team of Rhonda Black, Rachel Ippoliti, Lisa Fuller, Kim Johnston and Rochelle Jones (2013).

'BOYS ON HORSEBACK', WELLTOWN STATION, NSW, 1890S.
COURTESY DONALD MCLEOD CAMERON, AND THE RICHARD BUCHHORN COLLECTION.

INTRODUCTION

ABORIGINAL JOCKEYS — A PROUD PAST BUT AN UNCERTAIN FUTURE?

Aboriginal jockeys have played a small but vital part in the Australian racing industry since they first began riding in the nineteenth century. Yet the future for Aboriginal jockeys in Australian racing today is unclear, and seems only partly related to the current state and future of the industry itself. How can we explain the dramatic drop in the numbers of young Aboriginal riders pursuing careers as jockeys over the past three decades? What factors are at play, and what changes have occurred? This book explores the history of Indigenous involvement in racing over more than 150 years, and examines the evolution of this career path and the implications of a changing view of the involvement of Aboriginal riders in the industry.

From the nineteenth century through to the 1960s, many Aboriginal kids were given the opportunity to ride when they worked in the pastoral industry (see Frank Stevens and Ann McGrath). Their talent in the saddle, combined with their lack of capacity to secure employment elsewhere, made the stock industry one of the only means of subsistence available. Pastoralists quickly realised that Aboriginal people were not only great riders, but they knew the country intimately. Furthermore, their knowledge of living off and managing the land, and their understanding of the seasons, made them very valuable employees.

Over time, quite a few Aboriginal men graduated from the stock route to the racecourse and rodeo arena. Riders like Billy Waite, Harry Philips, Johnny Cadell (1950 Australian Bronc Riding Champion) and the man regarded as the greatest Aboriginal rough rider, Alec Hayden — who represented Australia in international rodeo test matches with Canada and the United States in 1937 — certainly made an impact on the rodeo circuit (see Tatz 1995). The accomplishments of these riders were achieved despite the quite rigid racial barriers that were endemic in white Australia during the period, making them even more remarkable. These barriers included the states' *Protection Acts*, which severely restricted people's movement and the choice of work they could undertake.

Although the move was intended to have a positive impact, the years after the introduction of award wages in the pastoral industry in 1968 saw a sharp decline in the numbers of Aboriginal people — men and women — employed by pastoralists and working as stockmen and drovers. Prior to this, Aboriginal people were paid little or nothing in monetary terms, receiving just food and clothing for themselves and sometimes their families. Sometimes even that money was held back through the 'protection' system, with only pocket money given to Aboriginal workers. This interrupted the previous flow of some of these young riders who had been taking their natural riding skills on to the racetrack.

The golden years of racing in Australia were between 1930 and 1960, when the Sport of Kings was unquestionably the nation's first national spectator sport. Racing — unlike any other sport, with the possible exception of boxing — offered unparalleled financial returns to those who enjoyed success in it. Athol George Mulley, one of the greatest Australian riders of any era, came out of his apprenticeship in the early 1940s with a small fortune of some £35,000.

In the late 1930s to early 1940s, as Australians struggled with the Great Depression, they were still happy to put their last coins on Phar Lap, who kept winning — in the process, becoming a national hero to the masses who flocked to the racetrack see him. Only cricket, with Don Bradman and the so-called Bodyline series of 1932–33, captured the public's imagination in the same way. These events highlight the rising element of Australian nationalism at the time. The uproar following the poisoning death of Phar Lap and the supposed duplicity of the Americans in his death, and the heightened Australia vs English competitiveness that Bodyline projected — akin to war — dominated the front pages of Australian newspapers. Growing up, I listened intently to stories my grandmother told me of 'how the Yanks poisoned Phar Lap' and how they followed news of Bradman batting against the Poms. Television was yet to be invented, and people visited the racetrack regularly for entertainment and to have a flutter.

Compared with other sports, racing offered an unparalleled opportunity for riders to reach dizzying heights of fame and fortune. The racetrack was where the press, politicians, movie stars and the elite of society could fete the leading jockeys. As an example, at the height of his stellar career, Darby McCarthy lived in a mansion in Chantilly, France with a French maid and a chauffeur-driven car. McCarthy was riding for the likes of the Wildensteins, Rothschilds and Prince Aly Khan. Nevertheless, for every outstanding successful jockey there were another thousand trying to eke out an existence on the dusty country bush circuit. Some had to take on additional work to supplement their income in order to support a family. These battling jockeys continued to live in hope of getting a mount on a champion horse that would catapult them into the limelight and provide financial prosperity.

Since the 1960s, Aboriginal people — especially men — have been encouraged into other sports, particularly Rugby League and Australian Rules Football (AFL). During the 1960s, the social and political changes that swept the globe had dramatic ramifications in Australia. The enforced barriers of the White Australia Policy were torn down and Aboriginal people began to attack the prejudice and long-buried guilt of white Australia. Seemingly for the first time, Australia began to feel the heat of an international gaze upon white settlers' appalling and discriminatory treatment of the country's Indigenous population.

Football codes opened their dressing room doors where previously racial barriers had prevented Aborigines from taking part. Aboriginal interest in the various football codes — and the financial returns on offer since — have seen great numbers of young Aboriginal kids pursue their dreams in the football stadium rather than on the racetrack. During the last 30 years, the glamour of the major football codes has witnessed a near-religious following within Aboriginal communities, enhanced by the trips to remote communities of some teams and football scouts seeking talented Aboriginal teenagers, whom they lure south or east.

It is hard to relate the special place that sport occupies in Aboriginal society, but Sean Gorman comes close in his book *Legends*:

> Sport was the only game in town, and for the majority it was Australian Rules, whether played on a dusty playing field, bitumen road or sports ground … where boys were encouraged to play football, where their uncles and families provided the role models; in some, where mothers took the boys to footy practice.

In recent decades, we have witnessed young Aboriginal footballers scale the highest levels within the AFL and Rugby League, commanding salaries in excess of $500,000 a season. In Rugby League, the success of the Indigenous All Stars has generated huge support for the pre-season opener, building on the long history of the Koori Knockout in New South Wales.

So what explains the drop in the number of young Aboriginal riders pursuing careers as jockeys? Prior to the 1960s, the lack of employment and access to regular quality food and nutrition were responsible for many young Aboriginal kids being under-nourished and carrying jockey weights. When my father, Merv Maynard, returned to Newcastle to start his apprenticeship aged only 13, he weighed a mere 4 stone 5 pounds (27.7 kilograms). When my grandfather died, my grandmother was left to feed five and survived on £3 a fortnight from St Vincent de Paul.

Another major factor since the 1960s has been the migration of thousands of Aboriginal people away from the rural sector, with its high unemployment rates, to more urban areas. During the years 1900 to 1960, many Aboriginal youngsters had opportunities to work in the pastoral industry, where their talent in the saddle and working for low wages delivered them some opportunity of employment. The years since have witnessed a dramatic drop of Aboriginal people working as stockmen and drovers, and this has probably had a backlash on some of these young riders then taking their riding skills to the racecourse.

In the aftermath of the 1967 Referendum, with the lifting of the stringent controls on Aboriginal people's movement, many sought new and what they perceived as better opportunities in the city. One negative outcome of that shift of families to the city in search of work was that Aboriginal kids were taken out of the bush and, for some, away from their long tradition of working with horses.

Additionally, since the 1960s, Aboriginal people have actively been encouraged into other sports — particularly Rugby League and AFL, where racial barriers once prevented them from taking part. The interest in the football codes and the financial returns have seen great numbers of young Aboriginal kids pursue their athletic dreams at the stadium rather than on the racetrack. Because Aboriginal kids now play football from a very young age, they bulk up early, making them too heavy to be riders.

Finally, racing crowds have been dropping for decades. The onset of a TAB in nearly every pub and club, and televised racing, have seen the track crowds dwindle to a trickle. The exceptions would be the big carnival meetings or the opportunity to see a once-in-a-lifetime horse like Black Caviar race. Aboriginal communities (along with many others) seem not to be attracted to visiting the track itself, or even working on and around it. The stable — where Aboriginal people traditionally worked — was always a hard life for jockeys and stablehands, and there are now more appealing alternatives available through other sports and through higher educational attainment. The Darby McCarthy Aboriginal Employment and Training Program — designed to provide Indigenous people with pre-vocational training, support and assistance to obtain and maintain a job, including traineeships and apprenticeships in the racing industry — may make some inroads in turning around this general drop of the quantity of young Aboriginal riders at the track. Only time will tell.

This book acknowledges and documents a fast-disappearing part of Aboriginal life and sporting history. Aboriginal people in the late 1960s revered legendary jockey Darby McCarthy, just as many Indigenous people do footballers Greg

Inglis and Adam Goodes today. The days of blackfellas heading to Randwick and putting their hard-earned money on any McCarthy mount are now just a memory. Sadly, one is left to lament the lack of a top-class Aboriginal jockey of the present era to once again grab the imagination of the racing public — black and white.

'HACKS AT WANGOOM' BY SAMUEL S KNIGHTS. COURTESY WENDY MCWHINNEY AND THE GEELONG GALLERY.

STOCKMAN, TURNER STATION, EAST KIMBERLEY, WESTERN AUSTRALIA, 7959. COURTESY CECIL WATTS.

PART I

BEHIND THE BARRIERS: THE BACKGROUND TO INDIGENOUS INVOLVEMENT IN RACING

THE ARRIVAL OF THE HORSE

The sight, sounds and smells of those magnificent animals from close quarters

Australia's first horses arrived in 1788 with the stallion, three mares and three yearlings that Governor Phillip had acquired at the Cape of Good Hope while en route to Australia. Within 20 years, this number had been boosted to 117.

Australian Indigenous people's first contact with the European animals was one of bewilderment and terror. Aboriginal people from the Gippsland area in Victoria thought that the noise of gunfire came from the horses' nostrils. The Kurnai of Gippsland thought they were huge dogs that would devour them all. On first encountering them, these terrified people struck camp and cleared out. Individuals from the Booandick people of south-eastern South Australia were terrorised from their sleep as they camped and thought of cattle as some kind of earthquake (literally 'thunder in the ground') or ghost.

Aboriginal people had good cause to fear the horse. Violent massacres and unprovoked vicious attacks were conducted from horseback. From his mission at Lake Macquarie, Reverend LE Threlkeld noted:

> Many Aborigines … were driven into a swamp, and mounted police rode round and round, and shot them off indiscriminately until they were all destroyed … men, women and children … Forty-five heads were collected and boiled down for the sake of the skulls.
>
> — *Gunson 1974*

Aboriginal skulls and other skeletal remains were highly prized by museum curators back in England at the time.

Although blameless for these atrocities, the horse gave the early settlers a decided advantage, providing mobility and speed over great distances. The violent nature of the frontier and the horse's role in it must have been a dramatic and frightening assault on the psyche of Aboriginal people. In a world that was changing dramatically around them, it was natural that they would want to gain knowledge and understanding of this new phenomenon, and within a short time they had shed their fears, displaying an open curiosity and an appetite to learn. Aboriginal culture was one that relied on an encyclopaedic knowledge and understanding of the flora and fauna of their environment for survival. They knew instinctively the behaviour and patterns of all the animals of their region.

Even as late as 1879 in the Kimberley region of Western Australia, Aboriginal people were both humoured and startled by the horse:

> They all roared with laughter when our guide explained to them that the gigantic animals (horses) were our willing slaves and could not talk, he told them about them carrying us long journeys, also our food. As soon as we got our saddles off the horses began to roll, the natives were spell bound

> for a while, then they threw themselves on the ground and again roared with laughter.
>
> — *Brockman 1987*

Eventually Aboriginal people caught horses and, using sheets of bark as makeshift saddles, taught themselves to ride. Settler accounts stated that Aboriginal people had an uncanny affinity with the horses, were excellent at looking after them and horse riding enchanted them.

They developed great skills as horsemen, were ambitious and did not mind a few falls. Work on horseback (particularly stock and bush work) was natural to them since they could adapt traditional knowledge and skills to European animals — sheep, cattle and horses. Aborigines became highly successful horse breakers as members of the native police, their skill as horsemen was complemented by their bush skills, making them a formidable adversary.

> The work of Aboriginal stockmen and women in building Australia is a story of terrible cruelty and injustice, of fortitude and adaptation, of great skill and quiet pride, all resulting in a huge-and almost entirely unacknowledged contribution to national prosperity.
>
> — *Wahlquist 1998*

The horse was incorporated into and identified in both Aboriginal language and art forms.

OFF AND RACING: CHARACTERS AND YARNS FROM THE INNER SANCTUM

ABOVE: 'THE SQUATTER'S TIGER', WATERCOLOURS BY ST GILL. BELOW: 'OUTWARD BOUND'. COURTESY MITCHELL LIBRARY, STATE LIBRARY OF NEW SOUTH WALES.

Aboriginal horsemen first ventured into horseracing as strappers and stablehands. Then they began to appear more frequently on the track — particularly in remote areas and at bush races. The *Illustrated Australian News* in 1891 describes a *Blackboys'* race in northern Queensland. Colin Tatz has highlighted similar events at Camooweal, Birdsville and Brunette Downs. Aboriginal jockeys were popular, for the best and fairest race was often fought out by these eager riders and sometimes the best horses were kept aside for the *Blackboys'* race. But although Aborigines rode many of the horses, they collected little of the prizemoney, socialised separately and were not allowed to buy beer. These races were presented for entertainment and amusement, and were obviously widespread. Commenting on his experiences, South Australian Aboriginal horseman Marty Dodd recalled:

> In those days [1920s and 1930s], you know, the Aboriginal lads, weren't allowed to ride … They had a race, what they called a *Blackboys'* race, at the end of the day.
>
> — *Dodd 2000*

Similar races were conducted in the Northern Territory:

> Organised horse racing began in the district in 1895 and was enjoyed by Aborigines and whites alike. Sometimes Aborigines were jockeys for whitemen in the main races, but there were also *Blackboys'* races'.
>
> — *Lewis 1997*

In 1835, an annual holiday race meeting was conducted near Fremantle in Western Australia on a cleared space at the back of town. The race meeting took on a festival atmosphere, and also featured other events such as wrestling, foot-races and wheelbarrow races, climbing greasy poles and chasing greasy pigs. Members of the local Aboriginal community were encouraged to attend. This was most likely because Indigenous people were viewed as curiosity items for the local settlers. However, the Aboriginal people upstaged their hosts. The little boys and girls raced for small prizes, the men ran for a purse and the Aboriginal people ran for loaves. An Aboriginal man called Migo so distinguished himself that he was afterwards pitted against the best runner among the white men and won by roughly a metre.

In the early days of organised racing in Australia, only a few jockeys were recorded as being Aboriginal. However, records reveal the presence of Aboriginal jockeys on major Australian tracks from the 1840s. An Aboriginal jockey called 'Sandy' rode successfully in Brisbane and Melbourne in the 1840s. He rode in the Melbourne Town Plate, the forerunner of the Melbourne Cup. Another

'A RACE WEEK UP NORTH' BY RG TAIT. COURTESY PICTURES COLLECTION, STATE LIBRARY OF VICTORIA.

Indigenous rider, simply recorded as 'Jackey', also won metropolitan races in Western Australia in the 1870s, including the Red Hart Stakes at Perth in 1877.

There remain some wonderful insights about Aboriginal jockeys buried in newspaper files:

> J Wallace, the stable jockey who steered Darkness to victory in the Hurdle race at Penola on Wednesday occupies a somewhat unique position, inasmuch as he is said to be the only member of his particular nationality extant. His father was a Chinaman and his mother an Australian [A]boriginal. Wallace is a fair horseman, and is by no means deficient in intelligence, and it was amusing to watch him as he came galloping home in front of the field. He wore a most expansive smile and looked at that moment one of the happiest beings alive.
> — *Border Watch, 14 March 1896*

> Darkness was ridden by 'Jackie' Wallace, whose colour was equally as black as that of the mare.
>
> Many old sports will, no doubt, remember the race, and very few will forget little 'Jackie' Wallace, who was a game and dashing rider and very popular …
>
> I met 'Jackie' some years ago, in 1920 to be exact, at Sandford, Victoria. He was riding a little old pony. His youth was a memory, but the master horseman was still there-great seat and hands …
>
> I am reminded when writing about 'Jackie' of another [A]boriginal jockey Bowman, well known as the rider of Reindeer, which I also saw compete on the old Narracoorte course. Bowman rode Reindeer in the Great Eastern at Oakbank, and after having completed three rounds of the course he turned to the judge's box and called out. 'How many more laps to go, boss?'
>
> — *Adelaide Chronicle, 14 September 1933*

Newspaper reports from the Wollongong area of New South Wales illustrate the success of Aboriginal riders:

> Traveller ridden by a Darkey took the lead and 'travelled' at such a rate that little Butterfly could not keep up with him.
> — *Illawarra Mercury, 1857*

> The Maiden Plate — first, Mr Thompson's 'Stranger' (Charley — [A]boriginal) … The riding of the 'blackfellow' excited much admiration.
> — *The Empire, 1857*

> Weight for age — Ladies Bracelet Third place — J. Ward's 'Countess' (blackfellow) The Two Year Old Stakes — First place C. Wright's 'Black Swan' (Charley — [A]boriginal).
> — *Young 2000*

Breaking through on the metropolitan tracks was not going to be easy. Carrying an Aboriginal identity would unquestionably attract unjustified criticism:

> The somewhat unusual spectacle on metropolitan courses of an [A]boriginal jockey having several mounts was witnessed at headquarters on Monday. Worrill, a native, rode for Mr. Roberts, of Yathro. While he had his mounts well forward early in the races he did not finish with any spirit or vigour.
> — *West Australian, 28 October 1903*

Records from the 1860s reveal that there was an Aboriginal camp very close to present-day Flemington, on the site of the tennis courts in South Yarra's Faulkner Park, near the corner of Park Street and Toorak Road.

BOOKMAKERS

Bookmakers and all forms of gambling were banned in South Australia in 1884 by an Act of Parliament. It was not until 1933 that the Betting Control Board re-licensed bookmakers to operate at racecourses and off-course betting shops and legal bookies reappeared on the racecourse.

This action initiated amendments to legislation, with two members of parliament suggesting that both women and Aboriginal people should be excluded from the new off-course betting shops. Women were to be excluded on the grounds that they should be kept on a 'higher plane' than men; Aborigines were to be excluded because they had a childish mentality. The two proposals were overwhelmingly rejected: one speaker who knew Aboriginal people well claimed that 'most were cleaner and whiter of heart than some politicians' (Lemon 1987).

IDENTITY, RACING AND RACISM

Thoroughbred horseracing was very much an elitist sport, the domain of bluebloods and those to whom they saw fit to allow admittance. Many Aboriginal people in pursuit of sporting dreams in football, boxing, athletics and other areas had been forced to adopt another identity to chase their dreams, free from persecution and with greater assurance that they wouldn't be denied opportunity. This was very much the same — and perhaps even more accentuated — within the confines of the class conscious 'Sport of Kings'. Horse racing saw many Aboriginal riders describe themselves as Islanders, Jewish, European or Indian in an attempt to gain the opportunity to ride and pursue their careers unhindered. Aboriginal riders were very much a part of the racing scene, but remained largely invisible to the population at large. Uncle Banjo Clarke reflected with sadness:

> In the early days, when Aboriginals became good at sport, they often had to pretend they came from another race — not Aboriginal. They had to register under a different nationality. Why was that attitude created?
> — *Clarke 2003*

Hardship and difficulties faced Aboriginal people, especially during the first six decades of the twentieth century. Obstruction to Aboriginal involvement in organised racing was referred to as a colour bar, but that colour bar only applied to people of Aboriginal descent.

The levels of stereotypical stigma and character assassination attached to an Aboriginal background over the course of those first five or six decades were — incredibly — founded in fear. For decades, Aboriginal people had been portrayed as relics of the Stone Age — a dying race, mentally inferior, unreliable, lazy, prone to the bottle and more than likely to up stakes and go walkabout without a moment's notice. The level of anguish, apathy and feeling of inferiority that this mental assault created in these people is probably incalculable. Its effects are still being felt today.

Aboriginal jockeys adopted different backgrounds as a way to gain riding opportunities. Jimmy Dries, a well-known bush jockey from the Gunnedah area, disguised his background in his pursuit of riding opportunities during the late 1920s. This practice of hiding identity had ramifications beyond the racecourse: when Jimmy's son, Doug, told of Aboriginal kids at school claiming to be cousins, his father replied that he was not Aboriginal — that the Dries were white and the kids at school were black. A perplexed Doug entered his bedroom and looked in a mirror. With his own reflection peering back at him, and with his father's words still ringing in his ears, Doug said to himself, 'Christ, dad's colour blind!'

Records indicate that Aboriginal jockeys certainly had barriers to overcome in many country areas:

> The proprietor of the Cleveland Racing and Trotting Club has decided not to allow the [A]boriginal jockey 'Albert' to ride again on the Cleveland course.
> — *Townsville Daily Bulletin, 10 February 1913*

> In response to an inquiry from the Broadsound Jockey Club, the secretary of the C.Q.R.A. (Mr. Tidbury) advised that it was not in the best interests of racing that an aboriginal should be allowed to ride as an amateur, and that the executive had not yet granted a jockeys license to an aboriginal.
> — *Central Queensland Herald, 5 May 1932*

The past levels of the racist, prejudiced, and xenophobic beliefs of wider white Australia make very unpleasant reading today:

> At times black boys (or gins) are given mounts at the races further back, and they cause quite a lot of amusement. I once saw a station gin dressed in fancy check shirt, neckerchief, sombrero and sheepskin chaps lead the way from barrier to box.
> When the race was over her husband abused her in the presence of the crowd because her mount had beaten his. He could not see that it wasn't her fault — that the flapping of the sheepskin chaps had really won the race.
> — *Sunday Mail (Brisbane), 1 September 1935*

Some media commentators did actually raise the question of why Australia had not produced greater numbers of Indigenous riders. But when one reads the content of the article, it becomes brutally clear that the barriers faced by Aboriginal riders were immense:

> Is it not rather remarkable that Australia has produced so few aborigines who made capable race riders? (says an exchange). With ordinary horses they are mostly quite at home, especially at station work and rough riding, but for some reason they are not in there element in the handling of the thoroughbreds in a race. There have been instances of half-castes showing skill and judgement on a racehorse probably the most notable of these having been Percy Kennedy. He was more than useful on the flat and over jumps when attached to the stable of the later Mr J.E. Brawer. Kennedy is now in charge of R. Lewis's property at Fern Tree Gully.

> In America several coloured men have achieved fame in the saddle, and it was there that the forward seat was first originated. Aborigines have excelled in other fields of sport, such as pedestrianism, but as jockeys they cannot be said to have gained much prominence. Perhaps they have not always been given the opportunity to learn, but we have seen a number of them working in racing stables in the old days, and they did not succeed when it came to riding in public. Probably they are mostly to dull witted to make expert jockeys.
> — *Western Mail (Perth), 19 April 1934*

The impact of social Darwinist theories of racial hierarchy were widely accepted on a global colonial scale:

> In commenting on the fact of coloured jockeys now being debarred from riding in Auckland Park (Johannesburg) a sporting scribe says the adoption of this course has eliminated much of the bumping in races, but whether this was entirely due to the lack of race-riding ability on the part of the coons it is hard to say. However, it is obvious that the barring of the coloured jockeys is proving a success.
> — *Warwick Examiner and Times (Qld), 3 June 1914*

In reading material like this, one is struck by the blatant sense of superiority and sickening contempt of the writers. One would like to think that the country has moved on from its racist historical past, but when we consider the 2005 Cronulla race riots, the opposition and barriers to asylum seekers from the north, mistrust and hysteria over Muslims and recent racist attacks against two of the highest-profile Aboriginal sports stars in the country, footballers Adam Goodes and Greg Inglis, one quickly realises that the racist fabric of the country is far from being a thing of the past.

Famed Aboriginal activist and sporting identity Charles Perkins recalled: 'Sadly in many sports Indigenous Australians simply haven't been given a go or barriers are placed in their way.' (Perkins 1999)

The dilemma faced by thousands of Aboriginal people during this period is worth closer study. For generations, Aboriginal people were subjected to policies and practices that denigrated their identity. The 1998 National Inquiry into the Separation of Aboriginal and Torres Strait Islander Children from Their Families found that many families 'exiled themselves from communities and hid their Aboriginal identity'. The fear of limited opportunities fostered the approach adopted by many, who cut off all ties with Aboriginal people — including other family members.

Many of the children taken from their families were brainwashed into feeling contempt and apathy for the Aboriginal people and their culture. This process is exemplified through some of the recorded memories of the Stolen Generations. Many of these children were placed with white families or simply institutionalised. They were taught to forget their identity, and to hate and fear any association or recognition with an Aboriginal background. There was to be no pride in being Aboriginal, only humiliation and anger:

> I didn't know any Aboriginal people at all — none at all. I was placed in a white family and I was just — I was white. I never knew, I never accepted myself to being a black person until — I don't know — I don't know if you ever really do accept yourself as being … How can you be proud of being Aboriginal after all the humiliation and the anger and the hatred you have! It's unbelievable how much you can hold inside.
> — *National Inquiry into the Separation of Aboriginal and Torres Strait Islander Children from Their Families 1997, p. 200*

The following archival sources reveal that horseracing was not exempt from the Stolen Generations experience. In 1907, a memorandum from Queensland's Chief Protector of Aboriginals to the Superintendent of the Aboriginal Home at Deebing Creek reveals an interesting twist and a connection with horseracing:

> An employer has applied to this office for four or five half-caste or quadroon boys between the ages of 12 and 14 years for stable work for service at Hendra and Sandgate. The wages offered are at the rate of 3 shillings per week each and clothing. Would any of the committed children be suitable?

The superintendent replied that there were three boys he thought 'would be suitable, Paddy, Jacky and Bundanda'. Mr Cox, the racehorse trainer who had initially sought the Aboriginal boys, wrote to the Chief Protector protesting their unsuitability, yet pleaded his case for them to continue at either a much reduced rate of pay or for nothing:

> With regard to the three boys taken out to Hendra yesterday; these boys are far too young and inexperienced to be worth any wages for the first year or two, and as you cannot apprentice them for a term of years, it would be useless for me to have anything to do with them and teach them to be thorough grooms and good boys with horses unless you were agreeable to allow them to sign on at the expiration of each year at the same rate of wages, namely 2 shillings per week.

The board replied, with little apparent concern for the welfare of the boys: 'So long as the boys are willing to continue in this service the Department will offer no objections.' In contrast, one of the boys' mothers wrote letters expressing how worried she was about him and wanting information. In the majority of cases, Aboriginal parents' correspondence to the authorities asking for information about their children was never answered. Elizabeth McKenzie Hatton, a white woman connected with the Aboriginal political movement of the 1920s, despaired that the Aborigines Protection Board ignored Aboriginal parents' cries for the return of their children:

> [D]ay after day letters come from the people, pleading for their children, asking me to find the girls, long lost to them — in service somewhere in this State — taken away in some cases over seven years ago and no word or line from them.
> — *The Voice of the North, 12 June 1925*

This intensive assault on Aboriginal culture and identity was a major reason why many Aboriginal people felt ashamed of the colour of their skin. Generations of Aboriginal people had to harbour this guilt and shame: to be identified as Aboriginal was to leave oneself open to persecution, denigration and prejudice. It has only been over the course of the past 40 years that the process of negativity fostered for decades has been disclosed, challenged and overthrown for its ignorance and outright hypocrisy. There remain many Aboriginal people who have only now begun the slow journey to regain their pride, dignity and culture.

ABORIGINAL WOMEN IN RACING

From the start of Aboriginal contact with the horse, women — like their male counterparts — displayed uncanny skill in the saddle. Aboriginal women's role in the stock industry has been poorly represented, and has often gone unrecognised. The Australian stockman is a rugged male, a pioneer, an individual and white. This is a potent and appealing image. It also totally obscures reality: most of our stockmen throughout history have been Aboriginal people, and many of them were in fact women.

The work of Aboriginal stockmen and women in building Australia is a story of terrible cruelty and injustice, of fortitude and adaptation, of great skill and quiet pride. All of it has resulted in a huge — and almost entirely unacknowledged — contribution to Australia's national prosperity. Without Aboriginal workers, the northern cattle industry and the billions of dollars in export earnings it has produced simply would not have developed. The underpaid — and often unpaid — labour of Indigenous people in conditions that were sometimes little better than slavery, their bush skills in tracking stock, their knowledge of the country and where to find water, and even the sexual services the women provided in those days were all vital to the cattle industry.

It has been asserted that the real Australian pioneers were Aboriginal women, because without them the white men could not have carried on. Aboriginal women were often preferred as stock workers because they were able to procure bush foods, and (just as importantly) they provided sexual services and female companionship. These liaisons included casual sexual exchanges similar to Western prostitution and harshly exploitative liaisons where women were imprisoned and raped. But there were also relationships that observed the complex and lengthy Indigenous protocols of arranged marriage.

Due to the racist attitudes and discriminatory legislation of the day concerning mixed unions, including child-removal policies, very few white men sought or obtained a legal marriage with an Aboriginal woman. Until the 1940s, there were laws against the races cohabiting or 'habitually consorting'.

Renowned Kimberley cattleman Matt Savage claimed that in the 1910s, half the stockriders in the area were Aboriginal women. Author Xavier Herbert said that white men would refuse to work on remote stations without available Aboriginal women — or what was termed 'black velvet'.

It was a cause of deep distress that both Aboriginal men and women were powerless to redress. White labour was not only difficult to obtain, but also often inferior in quality. Aboriginal people had remarkable skills in desert regions and showed considerable readiness for hardship and to risk their lives

GAYNOR CHAMBERS WITH HER TRAINER MOTHER, EMMIE WEHR, AND HER HORSE, STAR DANCER, AFTER WINNING A CLASS 3 HANDICAP. COURTESY GAYNOR CHAMBERS.

to aid an employer. In those days, Indigenous women were an integral part of the stock industry.

As a result of their horsemanship, Aboriginal women also dreamed of chasing careers as jockeys. Women of all persuasions were denied any licensed presence or recognised status in racing until 1978. Since then, however, hundreds of women have gained prominence as trainers and jockeys on Australian racecourses some like Gai Waterhouse have achieved outstanding success. It is highly likely that in many remote areas Aboriginal women had made an impact as riders well before 1978.

TO THE FINISH LINE

Every Aboriginal jockey throughout the history of Australian racing can be held up high as a beacon of Aboriginal achievement in a very intense, competitive and physically demanding sport. They have achieved untold success throughout the history of Australian racing. They have competed against the best in their profession, playing their part in the sheer exhilaration and excitement of Australian racing. Their stories vividly display them playing an active role through the pages of some of racing's most colourful and famous history.

The time of change for Aboriginal people was heralded during the 1960s. The decade proved a time of excitement and turmoil for the world: the escalation of the Cold War and the enormously divisive war in Vietnam, and the huge confrontation over civil rights for black America. None of this went unnoticed by Aboriginal people in Australia. They marched, protested, spoke out and wrote of both past and present injustices. To many people, the period seemed to mark the origins of black political consciousness in Australia. The Freedom Rides through New South Wales and the 1967 referendum finally acknowledged Aboriginal people as human beings. The establishment of the Aboriginal Tent Embassy on the steps of Parliament House in 1972 reaffirmed the suggestion of an awakening, organised and united Aboriginal political movement.

In retrospect, this was not the beginning of organised Aboriginal protest; rather, it can be likened to a phoenix rising. Certainly the Aboriginal political movements of the 1920s and late 1930s battled oppression, prejudice and assaults on the common rights of Indigenous people. The 1960s represented a welcome reignition of the spark that had been lit decades earlier and had overcome all efforts to douse or suppress it. In the sporting arena, Aboriginal Australians also became highly visible achievers. Lionel Rose was crowned world bantamweight champion and attracted bigger crowds in Melbourne than The Beatles. Evonne Goolagong captured Wimbledon and Darby McCarthy won the Epsom and AJC Derby in the one afternoon.

In the final analysis, Aboriginal involvement in the history of Australian horse racing is important. It reveals an area of Australian history that has been suppressed, denigrated or ignored across the past two centuries. That process is now being challenged and overthrown. Young Aboriginal people can also now draw strength and inspiration from their own heroes and heroines on the track.

The Aboriginal sporting presence in the new millennium is already reaching new levels of outstanding achievement, particularly on the football field with the exploits of Greg Inglis, Jonathon Thurston and Adam Goodes to name but a few, and through the charismatic and triumphant exploits of Olympic champion

THE WINNER AT THE VICTORIA RACING CLUB SPRING MEETING, *ILLUSTRATED SYDNEY NEWS*. COURTESY MITCHELL LIBRARY, STATE LIBRARY OF NEW SOUTH WALES.

Cathy Freeman on the athletic arena. Aboriginal jockeys are not out on the track in great numbers today, and we long for another Darby McCarthy to lead an Aboriginal racetrack renaissance and inspire a new generation of young Aboriginal kids to follow what is a long and proud tradition of great Aboriginal jockeys.

PART II
RIDING HIGH: THE STARS OF THE TURF

PETER ST ALBANS, 'SKETCH FOR PORTRAIT OF BRISEIS' BY FREDERICK WOODHOUSE. COURTESY RACING MUSEUM OF VICTORIA.

PETER ST ALBANS

Early morning trackwork, the smell of stables, hay, sweat, leather and molasses-laced feeds

TRIUMPHS
1876 AJC All Aged Stakes
1876 Australian Jockey Club Doncaster Handicap
1876 Melbourne Cup
1880 VRC St Leger
1880 Hobart Town Cup
1881 VRC Sires Produce
1881 Ascot Vale Stakes
1881 Geelong Cup
1880, 1881 and 1882 Geelong Mares Produce Stakes
1881 Geelong Sires Produce Stakes

Here we are at Randwick, in the autumn of 1876. The crowd cheers as the 12-year old Peter St Albans riding Briseis wins the Doncaster in one minute and 45.5 seconds. Briseis, carrying 5 stone 7 pounds [34.9 kilograms] clipped half a second off the race record.

Peter St Albans was a stable boy and strapper for James Wilson at St Albans' Stud near Geelong in Victoria. His first race ride (and winner), just prior to going to Sydney for the Doncaster, was when he rode the 2-year-old horse Newcastle to victory at Geelong in a Maiden Plate, winning by some 30 lengths. He was just 12 years of age.

St Albans was not booked to ride Briseis in the Doncaster; however, stable jockey Tom Hales — a leading rider of the era — could not make the weight. He pointed out to owner and trainer James Wilson that the young St Albans showed great ability as a horseman and had a special bond with the filly, and told Wilson to give the ride to young Peter.

Many ardent racegoers questioned Wilson's running of Briseis as a 2-year-old in the demanding Doncaster. It was a race for all comers over a mile, and would be ridden by an inexperienced boy. However, the win amply rewarded Wilson's confidence. Three days later, Briseis blitzed the opposition in the 6 furlong (1200 metre) Flying Handicap and the following day the filly's pairing with Peter St Albans, carrying 5 stone 11 pounds (36.7 kilograms) took out the All Aged Stakes over 1 mile (1.6 kilometres), where they defeated Kingsborough, one of the best horses in New South Wales at weight for age.

Seven months later, in the spring of 1876, a similar story unfolded at the Melbourne Cup. Although Tom Hales had ridden Briseis to victory in the Victoria Racing Club Derby on the Saturday in a record time of 2 minutes 43.25 seconds — the second fastest time ever recorded anywhere in the world — it was a different story for the following Tuesday's Melbourne Cup. Briseis was allotted 6 stone 4 pounds (39.9 kilograms), and again Hales could not make the weight. This time James Wilson needed no prompting, and without hesitation handed the reins to the now 13-year-old St Albans.

Stories relate that St Albans had to wag school to ride. On Cup Day, the principal of his Geelong school reportedly asked other students where young Peter St Albans was. His classmates informed the disbelieving principal that Peter was 'down in Melbourne winning the Cup'.

Peter St Albans and Briseis started at 7/1 and, before a crowd of 75,000 excited racegoers, Briseis comfortably won the Melbourne Cup by one and a half lengths in a time of 3 minutes 36.5 seconds.

Briseis and St Albans got away to a good start and were always handy to the leaders before the young jockey made his move at the distance. Briseis draws alongside Sybil and under strong riding proves too good over the concluding stages of the race. St Albans has ridden splendidly, sitting down and driving Briseis home in a manner that would have reflected credit on other more experienced jockeys.

It was considered that Wilson possessed a treasure in this lad. St Albans was afforded treatment equal to that of Wilson's sons, James and William:

> The St Albans stable has generally shown a peculiar style of riding, the inspiration of the genius and experience of Mr. J. Wilson. He trained his two sons, who were formidable lightweights, one after the other. As the second grew out of the register, he was replaced by St Albans, who proved himself up to the mark of the Wilson blood. If you have watched these three riders you will perceive that they have all been great on the finish – the rush on the post – the St Albans rush is the word. This involves a careful nursing of your horse until the critical moments.
> — *Brisbane Courier, 9 November 1882*

Briseis was the first filly or mare to win the Melbourne Cup. There were 33 runners in the race — the biggest field up to that time. The praise for the young jockey was ecstatic: Briseis was 'ridden by Peter St. Albans, who was a prodigy (one can use no other word)'.

Such was the strength of her Melbourne Cup win that two days later Briseis frightened off the opposition in the VRC Oaks so that only two horses opposed her. She won the race, this time with Tommy Hales in the saddle. Incredibly, she was again saddled up for the final day of the carnival, this time in the Mares Produce Stakes for 3-year-olds. But her winning run had ended. A tired and jaded Briseis battled on into second place, beaten by one and a half lengths by Pride of the Hills.

The following year, Peter St Albans came within a short half-head of winning the Melbourne Cup back to back.

The 1877 Melbourne Cup is best remembered as the occasion of one of the great race's most celebrated attempts to clean up the nation's bookmakers — the 'Savanaka Coup'. The main players in the coup were James Wilson, Herbert Power and Joe Thompson. James Wilson combined great horsemanship and training with shrewdness and an unrivalled ability to prepare a plunge on the bookmaking fraternity.

Herbert Power — one of Wilson's owners — was a high-profile owner desperate for racetrack success. He had owned the 4/1 favourite Feu d'Artifice, who had finished a disappointing fifteenth in the 1876 Melbourne Cup. Power exchanged Feu d'Artifice with Savanaka, a 2-year-old colt from prominent Bathurst breeder George Lee. The colt was a full brother to Kingsborough, one of the nation's top horses.

Savanaka had been entered in four races for 2-year-olds. His introduction to racing was in the Maribyrnong Plate, in which he was unplaced. In his second start, he won the 6 furlong (1200 metre) Flying Stakes and defeated top gallopers, including Pride of the Hills, Sultan, Tocal, Rapidity and Salisbury.

Wilson spotted something special in the win and set in motion one of the biggest betting plunges ever tried. First he convinced Power that they had a certainty, and they must not risk running him again for fear that the horse's true ability would be divulged to the racing world. Accordingly, he scratched the 2-year-old from his other engagements and sent him back to the St Albans' stud; the racing public quickly forgot him.

Wilson and Power hoped that with no real form to access, the handicapper would allot a light weight to Savanaka. When the weights for the Melbourne Cup were released the following year, they could be well pleased with this part of their objective. Savanaka was given a mere 6 stone 2 pounds (41 kilograms). Only four horses had received less weight, and Pride of the Hills — one of those beaten in the Flying Stakes — had been given 9 stone (57 kilograms).

The next stage was to 'get the money on'. It was a sensational week of betting. In one day alone, Savanaka was backed to win over £40,000 — the equivalent of an incredible $15 million today. The racing public's imagination was set alight. Nothing like the magnitude of this sort of betting had ever been witnessed — and it was all on a horse that had had only two starts and never been further than 6 furlongs (1200 metres). Adding spice to the situation, Chester — a horse trained by Melbourne Cup-winning maestro Etienne de Mestre — was also receiving heavy support. De Mestre had trained Archer, the winner of the first two Melbourne Cups. He was a 'conspicuous figure with his beard and velvet coat, he seemed to be always surrounded by a large team of horses and a retinue of Shoalhaven Aborigines' (Bernstein 1969). Chester had won the Australian Jockey Club (AJC) Champagne Stakes and Sires Produce, and ran what many thought was an unlucky second in the AJC Derby before heading south where he won the VRC Derby. After his Derby victory, his owner, the Hon. James White — Sydney's most successful owner — instructed his betting commissioner to place a wager with leading bookmaker Joe Thompson of £10,000 to £1000. Most reports state that the bet was only taken by Thompson because he believed that Savanaka was a certainty.

All that remained to complete the plot was to ensure that Savanaka was able to win the race. During training, the horse fully vindicated Wilson's early confidence. In a private trial at St Albans, he ran the Melbourne Cup distance of two miles in 3 minutes 33 seconds — incredibly, this was three seconds faster than the race record set by Don Juan (winner of the Cup three years before). Any doubts held by Power, Wilson or Thompson were dispelled.

Flemington was packed with excitement and drama. With 76,000 people on the course, the crowd was so dense that even the large grandstand known as Bagot's Cowshed was left with hardly enough room in which to move, and many people were injured in the crush. Then it rained: a torrential downpour that turned the ground into a quagmire, which was squelched beneath thousands of trampling feet. Jockeys were compelled to wear overcoats during the parades in the enclosure.

The race itself was full of excitement, with its start heralding the drama to come. When the flag fell, two runners — Robinson Crusoe and Amendment — were facing the wrong way and, in turning too quickly, collided, losing many lengths in the process.

From the jump the 100/1 bolter Fisherman sets up a blistering pace and is still leading when the field passes the abattoirs. Savanaka racing midfield is 'bolting under the proverbial double wraps behind Waxy'. But Disaster has struck. Fisherman has begun to tire and has dropped back through the field sharply. Waxy is unable to dodge the tiring Fisherman and falls. As Waxy falls in front of him, St Albans miraculously avoids the falling horse on Savanaka but in the process has virtually needed to pull him up to a stop. The incident has cost Savanaka at least ten to twenty lengths. Chester has avoided the scrimmage and comes into the straight contesting the lead with Glenormiston. Vagabond moves to second. We're now on the final furlong and Piggott who's riding Chester looks very relaxed almost as if he thinks the race is won. But St Albans on Savanaka bursts from the pack and charges down the outside, quickly overhauling Vagabond and failing by a mere half-head to grab Chester before the post.

They finished some three lengths clear of Vagabond in a new Melbourne Cup record of 3 minutes 33 seconds (exactly the same time as his trial) — one has to wonder what time Savanaka would have run except for the interference.

Though only a boy, Peter St Albans was applauded at having more than average talent in the saddle. He developed into a highly fashionable lightweight rider — even as an adult, he never weighed much more than 40 kilograms. He rode

Melita in the 1878 Melbourne Cup, starting as 4/1 favourite. He was recorded in the Australasian Turf register for 1880–81 as among Australia's principal riders.

St Albans rode Progress in the Melbourne Cup of 1880. In any other year, Progress would have been a great champion but the spring of 1880 was the time of the incomparable and unconquerable Grand Flaneur. St Albans and Progress finished second in the VRC Derby on the Saturday. They were second again on the Tuesday in the Melbourne Cup, beaten by a length. St Albans finished off a week of disappointment by running second on Constance in the VRC Oaks.

St Albans had been ill for some time prior to the 1880 Melbourne Cup. The press at the time recognised that although St Albans had not won the races, he had yet again proven his class, and that Progress had always been in a winning position had he been good enough. At 17 years of age, St Albans' record in the Melbourne Cup stood at a win and two seconds — an astonishing feat. Peter St Albans' public renown in the saddle continued to escalate.

> The autumn meeting of the Victoria Racing Club was commenced today at the Flemington course. The weather during the greater part of the morning was very cloudy and threatening, but by midday it cleared up, and was beautifully fine for the rest of the day. The attendance was rather meagre when the first race was run, but by two o'clock there was a considerable increase, and the reserve was very well filled … His Excellency the Marquis of Normandy, the Earl of Ellesmere, Lord Harvey Phipps, and Captain Patourel arrived before the first race was run and stopped till the end of the sport. The racing, on the whole, was not first class, except the Ascot Vale Stakes, which was perhaps the finest 2-year-old race ever run at Flemington … Eight youngsters faced the starter for the Ascot Vale Stakes, and as *Somerset* was thought to be the best of the St Albans lot, he was made favourite. He seemed to have the race in hand and be winning easily, when St Albans rushed *Royal Maid* out at the distance post, and won, after the most exciting finish seen on the course for many a day. The result was almost wholly due to the brilliant riding of young St Albans.
> — *Geelong Advertiser, 26 February 1881*

However, illness and serious injury from a fall in Sydney enforced St Albans' early retirement:

> Young St Albans, the favourite jockey of Mr Jas. Wilson's stable and who was so seriously injured at the races in Sydney a couple of weeks since arrived in Geelong by the midday train from Melbourne yesterday. He appears to have received a severe shock to the system, but although rather

weak, he was able to walk from the railway carriage to a cab in front of the station.

— *Geelong Advertiser, 27 April 1882*

He later became a horse trainer. His best horse was Forest King, who he prepared for GH Upjohn. In 1891, Forest King ran third in the Geelong Cup, won the Geelong Winter Handicap and ran second to G'naroo in the Caulfield Cup.

Peter St Albans died at the age of just 35 in 1898, at the Breakwater home of his father-in-law, William Ryan. He was survived by his wife Anastasia, and by all accounts the funeral was one of the largest ever seen in Geelong. However, no headstone or monument marks his grave, and there is no marked account or record of his burial at the cemetery:

> There was a large assemblage of sporting men at the funeral of late Mr Peter Bowden (Peter St Albans), which took place yesterday afternoon. The cortege was a lengthy one, the hearse being followed to the place of internment, the Eastern Cemetery, by two mourning coaches and 50 private and public conveyances, and several horsemen. The floral tributes were numerous and beautiful, and among them were two from St Albans, one from Mr Jas. Wilson sen., tied with the racing colours of that gentleman; others from Mr and Mrs Sparrow, and Mr and Mrs Hugh Munro; an everlasting cross from Mr Hocking's employees; floral wreath, Mr and Mrs Armour; floral crescent, Mr Chris Moore; floral anchor; Mrs Jackson. The following gentlemen acted as pallbearers: Messrs Jas. Wilson, sen., Hugh Munro, Chris Moore, Bert Morrison and H. Naim. The Rev Father Foughey officiated at the grave and Messrs Stephen Wellington and Bros. carried out the Mortuary arrangement.
>
> — *Geelong Advertiser, 26 July 1898*

It seems strange there is no mention of the Bowden family — other than Peter himself — in the funeral notice.

PETER ST ALBANS: ABORIGINAL OR NOT?

Since writing this section back in 2002, there have been a number of revelations claiming to solve the mystery and identity of the young boy known as Peter St Albans who captured the 1876 Melbourne Cup. I am not convinced that full closure on the identity of Peter St Albans has been achieved, and I seek to answer some of the controversy that has arisen.

Back in 2002, I stated that the racial background of Peter St Albans remained uncertain but his accepted surname was indicative that he was possibly Aboriginal. I want to state up front that it is not and has never been my intention to claim Peter St Albans was Aboriginal. What I said back in 2002 regarding St Albans' identity was that it was shrouded in mystery and may never be resolved. I still maintain that understanding:

> A number of references attest that 'Peter St Albans was taken as a boy by Mr. J. Wilson, Sen., and was named after the St Albans training establishment.
> — *Barrier Miner, 12 August 1895*

In my original study, I pointed out that Aboriginal people were very often assigned the names of their 'owners', or of the homesteads and stations where they worked — a thing that rarely (if ever) occurred among non-Aboriginal people. An article in the *Melbourne Argus* a week after Briseis won the Melbourne Cup is even more revealing:

> Some years ago the boy was wandering about the streets of Geelong a friendless waif, when Mr Wilson, with that kindheartedness for which he is so well known, took him home, fed, clothed and adopted him. Not only did he do this, but as the little fellow was totally ignorant of his parentage on either side, Mr Wilson bestowed upon him the aristocratic name of his own residence, St Albans, taught him to ride, and one of the results is that the lad, with the help of the game filly Briseis landed for his master the rich racing stake in question.
> — *Melbourne Argus, 16 November 1876*

I also stated in 2002 that the painting by Frederick Woodhouse had done little to settle any dispute: it features Peter St Albans standing alongside Briseis with stable jockey Tom Hales in the saddle (although some analysts have argued that St Albans appeared white or European in the picture). Other stories attest that St Albans was left as a newborn baby on the doorstep of one of the stud grooms. The baby was believed to have been the result of a secret love affair between one of the stablehands and a housemaid at the Wilson homestead. He was subsequently raised by the stud groom and his wife, and given the name St Albans.

However, many people believed — and racing legend as related by Robert Windmill dictates — that either James Wilson or his son was in fact Peter St Albans' father, and that his mother had likely been an Aboriginal domestic servant. James Wilson was devoted to and unashamedly enraptured with Peter St Albans. This was highly unusual for a man with a merciless and uncaring reputation with jockeys.

The story, as it went, stated that one of James Wilson's employees, Michael Bowden, and his wife were paid to raise Peter St Albans as their son, in effect disguising Wilson's apparent lack of discretion. The Bowdens themselves were not of Aboriginal descent. When a fire destroyed the home of Michael Bowden at St Albans' stud in June 1876, James Wilson paid for a new house to be built. Bowden was only a stablehand and labourer of the establishment, and meant absolutely nothing to Wilson. But the Bowdens were the family entrusted to raising Peter St Albans and looking after his welfare, and this was his residence and home. While it is quite possible that Wilson's payment may have been the action of a generous man catering to a poor family in need, it may also have been the action of a concerned father for his son.

So many stories and possibilities! I think the truth is buried some where in between that of waif, illegitimate child and legitimate son of the Bowdens.

I was able to reveal what little evidence has been put forward on the relationship between the Wilson family and Aboriginal people. However, a newspaper account in the *Hamilton Spectator* revealed that Wilson's brother Joseph was prepared to speak out on the treatment of Aborigines even in the face of ridicule and derision.

Joseph Wilson was a successful businessman and active member of the local council and political electorate of the Hamilton area in Victoria. In 1861, he attended a meeting held at the Victoria Hotel where the newly elected representative of Dundas, a Mr Mollison, addressed the gathering. Mollison was obviously well liked and had the support of the parochial crowd. Wilson spoke out at the meeting against what he felt was wrong. For his outspokenness, Wilson earned the ire and jeckles of the crowd.

'Got the black book, Joe?' the crowd interjected.

Mollison, playing to the crowd, taunted Joseph.

'I cannot agree with a man who has only been landed a short time in the colony being considered equal as regards a vote to one who has been a colonist for years,' he jeered.

The crowd roared and cheered its approval, but Wilson would not be silenced and retorted that Mollison was not 'a fit and proper person' to hold office. In conclusion, he declared that he did not care whether they laughed at him, as he was well aware of how they had robbed the blackfellow of his land. His final defiance was met with only increased laughter.

Like his brother, Joseph Wilson also had an illegitimate child (although not Aboriginal) about whom he agonised and felt responsible. He eventually adopted the girl, showing his guilt and compassion for his transgression.

In 2002 I noted that consensus from numerous studies conducted over many decades by racing historians, journalists and academic scholars, including Bernstein, Ahern, Cavanough, Pollard, Tatz, Ryan and Windmill, concluded that Peter St Albans was Aboriginal. More recent studies since then have questioned the strength of the earlier works. The accuracy of earlier studies — mine included — has been questioned. Two publications have gone so far as to argue that the identity of Peter St Albans has now been finally and conclusively established.

Firstly, noted racing journalist Max Presnell, in an article in November 2004, announced that 'Peter St Albans, one of the most fascinating names in Melbourne Cup folklore, wasn't Aboriginal. And that's not going down the prejudice track. "He was indeed Peter Bowden and the son of Irish parents," Father Peter Rankin, the long-term parish priest at Kilmore in Victoria and a direct descendant of St Albans, related. "And I don't tell lies".'

Presnell went on to disclose that Father Rankin's sister, 'Nola Hyde, a sprightly 80-year-old and in charge of the family archives, was happy to relate the bloodlines that would, for clarity, do the *Stud Book* proud.'

> 'When you say he's not Aboriginal you make it sound racist but it's the last thing I want,' she stressed. 'After all, they were here before us anyway. I'm happy if he was Aboriginal because it would mean we would have Aboriginal blood in us, but we haven't.'

Back in 1998, when I spoke to Nola Hyde, she raised the same point with me: 'We are not Aboriginal' — a point with which I totally agreed. The St Albans riddle for me was far more complex than that, however.

Presnell stated that Nola had revealed that 'Peter was too young to ride in the Melbourne Cup as he was only 12', so at the time they argued that his birth date and parents were unknown, thus allowing him to ride in the Cup. But in those days there was no restriction on the age for jockeys. If you were good enough, you were legged up. For example, Jim McHugh was aged only 11 when he won the 1897 AJC Epsom on Robin Hood. Sid Ferry was 10 when he won the Adelaide City Handicap in 1888. The famous Wooten brothers, Frank and Stanley, were aged 9 and 11 respectively when they first started riding.

The major revelation in the Presnell article was that the family now suggested that Michael Bowden Junior was in fact Peter St Albans. If so, he would have been younger than the recorded age of Peter during his Melbourne Cup and Doncaster victories. I am not convinced that they were the one and the same. If Peter was in fact Michael, why did he not revert to his own name at the time, and why was it not noted at the time of his death? Why in 1879, when there was no need for pretence, did Peter sail to Sydney on board the *Barrabool*, accompanied by Mr Wilson Jnr under the name Peter Albans?

When I spoke with Nola, there was no mention of Michael Bowden being Peter. As far as I am aware, there is no record of the family raising this in any previous correspondence. The family may have uncovered new material — which would explain this change of course — but as far as I am aware, this is not the case.

Just after I had spoken on an ABC TV *Hindsight* program on Aboriginal jockeys back in 2009, Andrew Lemon contacted me in his capacity as a consultant historian for the Victoria Racing Club (VRC). Andrew raised some concerns on an online site and subsequently via email with me regarding his new study concerning Peter St Albans. I was able to highlight that the age of jockeys riding at that time would not have necessitated a need to camouflage the young rider's real name.

Next, in 2011 Andrew Lemon presented the Don Grant Lecture at the State Library of Victoria, published as *Storming the Barricades – the Family History Revolution*. Lemon's study presented a much more in-depth attempt to solve the mystery of Peter St Albans' background. At the start of his address, he stated his aims and directives:

> My tale is of how a boy born in Geelong of Irish parents whose names were Michael and Catherine and came from County Cork and Tipperary respectively, was transformed by folk lore into an Aboriginal orphan, illegitimate love child of a station owner; a 13-year-old who wagged school and won Australia's greatest race, the Melbourne Cup; and of how difficult it has been to reassign him to his correct family, his correct age and his correct place in history. I am as certain now as a historian ever can be that his parents were indeed Irish and lawfully wed, that he had his own name and knew exactly who he was, that he grew up part of his large Irish Australian family, and that when he won the Melbourne Cup he was not 13 but 11 years of age.

Andrew also pointed to a newspaper reference describing St Albans as a 'freckle-faced lad', thinking that this was evidence that he was not of Aboriginal descent. I informed Andrew that I had seen the very same reference back in the late 1990s, but over decades of working in every state and territory of this country with our communities — urban, rural and remote — I have also seen Aboriginal people right across this country covered in freckles!

Andrew Lemon is indeed correct in noting that there was no St Albans' Stud or training establishment when Peter was born, and for him to be named after at the time. But he wasn't named after the establishment at the time of his birth — it was bestowed upon him when he was reportedly taken in as a young boy.

A major focus of Lemon's argument centres on David Lee Bernstein's social history of the Melbourne Cup, *The First Tuesday in November*. Lemon rightly argues that later writers, including Ahern, Windmill, Pollard, Tatz and myself, had largely relied on Bernstein's work and had not examined or questioned his findings in greater detail. It was Bernstein who first drew attention to Peter St Albans having an Aboriginal background.

Bernstein's interview with Mrs Nancy Dexter lies at the heart of the idea of St Albans being Aboriginal. Mrs Dexter's grandmother went to school with Peter St Albans at the Lake Coonewarre School in 1876, and apparently claimed that Peter was Aboriginal. Lemon berates that Bernstein does not source these details properly. Lemon then argues that 'Bernstein is telling a second-hand story, by now more than ninety years old. It is Bernstein's words (not those of Nancy's grandma) we hear: "he was an aboriginal, and, like many such waifs, had no patronymic".' It seems Andrew is prepared to accept the family history knowledge passed down to the Bowden family, but as apparently not that passed down in the Dexter family.

Mrs Nancy Dexter (1923–86) was arguably a relatively reliable informant. She was a very prominent and respected newspaper journalist who wrote for *The Age* during the 1960s, 1970s and early 1980s. A women's liberation advocate before the term had even been coined, she wrote articles on such contentious issues as equal pay, domestic violence and abortion law reform. She also had a great interest in horse racing, and married Harry Dexter, a Melbourne-based racing writer with the Sydney *Sun*. Harry was 22 years older than Nancy when they married in 1951, and was from a very well-known family of racing writers. So she was possibly not just relying on her grandmother's memories of Peter St Albans at Connewarre School, but also her husband's family's extensive local racing history knowledge.

In his detailed history of the Geelong Racing Club, Robert Windmill had much to say about the trainer James Wilson and his jockey, Peter St Albans. It was Windmill who first canvassed the story that St Albans was the illegitimate son of James Wilson. Lemon stated that Windmill's sensational revelation was from unsourced local stories:

> Windmill was floating a theory of his own to fit what he understood to be the existing facts. In his research into James Wilson, he had heard unpublished gossip about the wealthy trainer, who (and this is on the record) late in life, as a widower, married his housekeeper.

Lemon next took issue with my own work:

> Through his special study, John Maynard was trying to claim recognition for Indigenous pride. Here it must have seemed I was out to steal Peter St Albans back from an Aboriginal background: and this in the context of what media and academics were both calling the 'History Wars'.

Andrew Lemon presents himself as motivated purely by the quest for historical truth:

> historical truth is my objective, however difficult it is to find in practice. And why is it important? Because, in this case for instance, Peter St Albans is an individual in history, a real person who deserves the truth, as closely as we can find it.

Lemon has uncovered a gem of information while searching Trove (mentioned earlier in this study):

> Some years ago the boy was wandering about the streets of Geelong a friendless waif, when Mr Wilson, with that kindheartedness for which is so well known, took him home, fed, clothed, and adopted him.

This discovery caused some consternation. 'Was Bernstein right after all?' Lemon described his own inner interrogation:

> No mention here of Aboriginal. Naturally no mention of Wilson as the father. So what do we make of it? This is the *Argus* quoting verbatim the *Clunes Guardian*. Why Clunes? Neither Wilson nor Peter, to my knowledge, had any connection with the gold town north of Ballarat. What's interesting is that a few papers took up this story in the days following, word for word, attributed to the *Argus* or the *Clunes Guardian* but it went no further. It was not carried by the *Geelong Advertiser*. Unlike the Bernstein story, it never gathered pace. The reason has to be (and here I wave the 'I am speculating' flag) that it wasn't true: that James Wilson had been pulling the leg of a gullible reporter asking a nosy question …

Of course, there is no mention of being Aboriginal or that James Wilson was the father. Why would there be? In relation to Clunes, the gold town north of Ballarat, I noted in my earlier 2002 book that James Wilson's brother was a successful businessman, and member of the local council and the political electorate of the Hamilton area of Victoria. Joseph Wilson obviously moved widely across the area and may well have been a source of information. As anyone who has any knowledge of James Wilson would testify, the trainer wouldn't bother pulling anyone's leg. He was renowned for not talking to the media.

Lemon explains that during this period racing was under investigation because of criminal activity, and this might have been the reason why Peter St Albans' name was changed.

Wilson sought to protect the identity of this very young, talented boy to prevent bookmakers or betting men getting to him or his family with bribes, threats or inducements.

It is unlikely that a name change would have protected the young rider from being contacted by underworld and criminally connected bookmakers. Wilson himself was connected with one of the most celebrated bookmakers in Australian racing history, Joe Thompson. Throughout his career, Thompson was connected with more rorts and skulduggery than most. Peter St Albans himself is not free from some historical rumour, innuendo and intrigue over the poor performance of a Melbourne Cup runner. In 1887, Meteor started favourite in the Melbourne Cup, but:

> was one of the first horses beaten. Although ordinarily a quick beginner and a free galloper, Meteor on this occasion was outpaced from the jump, and beat only one horse home. After the race it was asserted that Meteor had been got at, and all sorts of rumours were flying about. To this day Mr. Maitland declares that Meteor was drugged, and that the horse showed all the signs of narcotic doping. How the dope could have been administered is difficult to conceive for Peter St. Albans slept in Meteor's box and the horse was never left, day or night.
> — *Gippsland Times, 25 March 1918*

Lemon returns to the Bernstein book and notes that the VRC had provided Bernstein with letters written by descendants of the Bowden family. Maureen Knight wrote:

> As there appear to be many conflicting stories in published texts as to the identity of a particular jockey, namely, Peter St Albans, jockey of the 1876 Melbourne Cup winner, Briseis, and as an interested descendant of 'Peter St Albans', I would like to make a correction to this information for your future records and for any further publications. It has only been in recent years that his family have become aware of certain claims. 'Peter St Albans' was, in fact, Peter Bowden. The Bowden family lived at St Albans stables and each day Peter would go and help with the horses.

There is no mention of Peter being Michael in this correspondence. Lemon also refers to a letter written by Bernstein to descendants of the Bowden family, dated 15 February 1970. Bernstein confesses to an error on his part:

> I am indebted to you and your sister for drawing attention to my error in FIRST TUESDAY IN NOVEMBER in stating that Peter St Albans, who won the Melbourne Cup on Briseis in 1875 [he meant 1876] when only 13, was an aboriginal.

Bernstein, sadly, was not a meticulous researcher. He did not question the Bowden families' revelations, nor did he return to his original source with Nancy Dexter for further interrogation. When told that Peter was in fact a Bowden, he left it at that — and an opportunity was lost.

Andrew Lemon does acknowledge the Bowden 'family history sources, in all their glorious contradictions'. First, there is the problem that if Michael Jnr was Peter St Albans, then his birth date did not correspond to that given on the death certificate of Peter St Albans. The only consistency in the Bowden family history, as Lemon states,

> is that Michael senior was born in Cork, his wife Catherine (not Cathleen), nee Carmody, in Tipperary and that they were married in Geelong in 1854. They had certainly one, probably two children who died at birth or soon afterwards, and they reused these names for later children. On some of the later family lists the name of Peter (or Michael 1864) is missing.

Lemon's major find and piece of evidence, a Probate file held in the Public Records Office, concerns a family dispute. It does not relate to Peter, but rather to Michael Bowden Senior. Apparently the elder Bowden left no will when he died in 1890, and there was a difference of opinion over the outcome. Lemon states:

> The document adds new evidence (probably 'facts') to the family information in the form of affidavits by Kate and Roderick [children of Michael Bowden Snr]. The first surprising claim (since there had been no mention on any of the family certificates) was that there was an eldest son, John, living at the Kensington near Melbourne. The affidavit said he came from an earlier marriage — even though Michael Bowdren, the father, had been described as a bachelor when he married Catherine Carmody in 1854. The third fact was that the man customarily known as Peter in his family, and called Peter on his marriage and death certificates — the Peter we are talking about — is described formally in this document as Michael Bowden (horse trainer), deceased. Sister Kate, aided by a good lawyer, has been careful with such detail in the documents — all of which consistently name the father as Michael Bowdren, with the 'r', as distinct from Michael Bowden a.k.a. Peter, the son. This important linkage confirms that the boy Michael Bowden, birth registered in November 1864, was one and the same as Michael Bowden, horse trainer, deceased, who was without

question one and the same as Peter Bowden, horse trainer previously known as jockey Peter St Albans. I would also observe that if Peter had not been a legitimate part of the Bowden family, Kate would have had every motive in this case to denounce him as a ring-in. She did not do so.

Lemon understandably assumes that, since Michael Bowden is described formally in the document as a former horse trainer, then it must be Peter, as it had been believed Peter was the only former jockey and trainer in the family. But new information overthrows that analysis.

In June 1882, two South Australian newspapers, the *South Australian Advertiser* and the *South Australian Victuallers Gazette*, give coverage to an exciting local racecourse announcement. A brother of Peter St Albans, himself a former jockey and stable lad with James Wilson, had relocated to Adelaide to set up a training establishment:

> Frank Musgrove, who was recently with Henry Tothill, has entered into a partnership with a brother to Peter St Albans named Bowden, for eight years in the service of J. Wilson near Geelong, and the pair have taken the commodious stables adjoining the Parkside Hotel, where they are prepared to take in horses to train. At present their string is limited to three, but as the renowned little Peter, the rider of Briseis in the Melbourne Cup, and many other famous winners will join the firm after finishing his apprenticeship in August next, the attraction of such a competent horseman will doubtless speedily lead to an increase of patronage.

This announcement completely alters the evidence in the probate report revealed by Andrew Lemon. It could not have been Roderick (who was a policeman — too big for a jockey) and it could not have been John (who was unknown to the rest of the family before the affidavits). I believe that the brother who had just relocated to Adelaide was actually Michael Bowden Jnr. If that is the case, we are back to square one in relation to Peter St Albans. Naturally, if Peter was not a biological son, other family members did not include him — unlike Michael — in the probate discussion.

Unfortunately, the brother in Adelaide is neither mentioned by first name or initial. I have perused shipping records, but so far have not been able to come up with a record. However, this brother probably arrived in South Australia on 29 April 1882 on board the ship *Victorian*, still employed by James Wilson Snr. Newspaper coverage reports revealed that the ship carried a number of horses that were to run in the South Australian May carnival:

> Amongst them were the St Albans team, comprising Hereford Bay, Royal Maid, and Belmont in the care of J. Wilson Jun and W. Wilson and they are now located at the Parkside Hotel.

Evidently, Bowden the brother did not return to Victoria with the St Albans team, but stayed on in the same stables and entered into a training partnership with Frank Musgrove. A few further reports of the pair paid glowing testament to their training methods: 'Musgrove and Bowden deserve praise for the style in which they work their horses. Intrepid never looked better'; and 'Musgrove and Bowden gave Intrepid some slow work for 6 miles'. Success was not forthcoming, however. The much-heralded arrival of Bowden's fabled brother Peter St Albans did not eventuate. Peter, of course, had been seriously injured in a fall off Royal Maid in Sydney in April, and although he did return to the track, he never recaptured his former glory and was forced to retire. That Michael Bowden Jnr was a jockey and a trainer is correct, but he is not Peter St Albans.

Andrew Lemon's one other piece of evidence for his theory is an article in the *Otago Witness* of 26 November 1881 stating that when Catherine Bowden died in late October 1881, near the start of the Flemington spring racing carnival and with the Melbourne Cup running on the first Tuesday of November, 'Peter St Albans did not ride through the meeting owing to the death of his mother.' Lemon provides this as evidence that Peter was the biological son of Catherine. As the father of five children, the middle son of whom is in fact my stepson, I disagree with this analysis. If Peter Bowden had known no other mother than Catherine, it is completely irrelevant whether she was his biological mother or not. He clearly loved her as his mother — unquestioned!

There have been many speculations about the background of Peter St Albans, and I will put forward another. To name the more prominent, it has been assumed that he was a baby dropped at the property; that he was the illegitimate son of James Wilson; that he was the son of Catherine and Michael Bowden. Yet Andrew Lemon has brought to light information that Michael Bowden Snr was in fact the father of another child from a previously unknown marriage. What if Michael Bowden Snr was the father of Peter St Albans and another woman was the mother? Through Lemon's work, we also know that the Bowdens lost at least two children at a very early age. Catherine Bowden may well have been willing to take in another child to replace these losses. Adding to this line of thought, there is an Aboriginal Bowden family from Victoria. In 1922, driven to write a response to an article Daisy Bates wrote in the *Sydney Morning Herald*, misguidedly describing Aboriginal people as cannibals and savages and asserting that Aboriginal women were ill-treated, an Aboriginal woman named Annie Bowden wrote:

> The women were always taken care of in my case, and made much of; there was more discipline in the camps than there is in many white homes today … Boys were taught from earliest infancy to respect their mothers and their sisters, and no one woman had more than one husband. She states that all Aboriginal dialects throughout Australia have terms only for the lowest, such as lying and cheating and thieving, and no terms [for] honesty, making the language in common with the rest as low as she possibly can. It would be laughable if it were not so serious; and we know it is not true. I am an [A]boriginal and understand and speak eight different languages. I am an educated woman, having been educated in the State schools of Victoria and I think I am in a better position to know than a white woman.
>
> — *Sydney Morning Herald, 20 May 1922*

In 1922, Annie Bowden was living at La Perouse Aboriginal community in Sydney, having come up from Victoria. So we have a Bowden Aboriginal family that ties to the same time period in Victoria as Peter St Albans and the non-Indigenous Bowden family. It may not link, but in family history anything is possible, and Michael Bowden Snr may well have sired Peter — and some other Aboriginal offspring into the bargain. This was fairly common at the time.

In conclusion, much mystery still remains concerning the story and identity of Peter St Albans, and it may never be resolved. At the end of his address, Andrew Lemon referred to the song 'Bring Him Home' from *Les Miserables*, stating that it stirs the heart-strings and that he 'would like to say to Peter St Albans, Peter Bowden, champion Australian jockey: welcome home'. For me, this rendition of the triumphant song (or at least its intent) might have been slightly premature. What is indisputable is that Peter, whatever his identity may prove to be, was an outstanding jockey. His story is a crucial one in the annals of Aboriginal racing history, and he remains forever unequivocally tied to the Bowden family.

RAE 'TOGO' JOHNSTONE

Cracking whips

TRIUMPHS
One of the most celebrated international Australian riders
Won more than 3000 races in nine countries with a total of 36 classics

Nervous and temperamental — almost to the point where he had the shakes before he got on a horse — Rae Johnstone had no time for foolishness, either from importunate reporters or from careless grooms. Once on the track, he was in command, coaxing and steadying flighty horses, always ready with a calming pat. Rae Johnstone was arguably Australia's most successful international jockey. His remarkable riding career took him to Europe, where he married a beautiful woman, rode horses for the Aga Khan, was locked away as a prisoner of war and rode winner after winner after winner.

Johnstone died in 1964 and went to his grave without revealing anything other than superficial observations of his young life.

Rae Johnstone was born in 1905 at Newcastle, New South Wales. As a young boy, he moved to Sydney with his mother. At that time, his dreams lay in becoming a star Rugby scrum half, but the fact that he tipped the scales at a mere 4 stone 7 pounds (29 kilograms) was hardly a good start for this career. On one occasion, his father visited and took him to a race meeting at Canterbury — an intoxicating experience. He just 'got drunk on the atmosphere' (*Daily Mirror*, 15 May 1989), and decided there and then to become a jockey.

The move to Sydney — especially to Randwick and Kensington in the city's Eastern Suburbs — was opportune. He attended Marist Brothers College at Darlinghurst, where his best friend was Cyril Angles. Angles belonged to one of the most famous Australian racing families of the twentieth century and was instrumental in introducing his mate Rae to horses when he allowed the youngster to ride the Angles family pony all over the district.

In Randwick and Kensington, Johnstone had ready-made horse-mad kids with whom to compete. Among the other youngsters who rode their ponies in improvised races and over makeshift hurdles on Payten's Paddock — later to become part of Avoca golf links — were Jim and Darby Munro and Mick Heynes (who would become a hurdle jockey).

Johnstone was introduced to Jack Phoenix and, against his mother's wishes, he joined the Phoenix stable. He rode his first winner, Grey Arrow, at the age of 15 at Canterbury, much to the delight of his mother who had invested £10 each way on her son. It was her first-ever bet.

From the outset, Johnstone was a rare if impetuous talent. He was flamboyant, cocky and imbued with self-confidence in his horsemanship and skill. In this he was well ahead of his time: it was not customary for jockeys of the period to demonstrate and declare openly on their own ability. In his first full season in the saddle (1922), Johnstone rode more than 100 winners and earned his first nickname of 'Tiger'. At the age of 17, he defeated Jim Munro and secured the Sydney apprentice jockeys' premiership.

Unfortunately, Johnstone had also become a compulsive and reckless gambler. He arranged to bet illegally on his own mounts through an intricate system of signals as he went out on to the track. He stationed friends at various points around the enclosure to observe his actions, and it was not long before his activities drew the attention of the stewards. When they saw the bank account held in trust for him by his mentor, they discovered that he had gambled away his entire earnings. Johnstone was banned from riding in Sydney and was not allowed to ride within a radius of 160 kilometres of the metropolitan area.

Many young riders dropping out of the big time would have despaired of ever regaining a spot back in the upper echelon. But Johnstone re-established himself in the southern districts and fought his way back to the top by sheer numbers of winners and a string of country successes. On his first day back riding in Sydney, he rode four winners. He was also hospitalised for an operation on his appendix and met his first wife, Ruby. However, back on the track he was constantly under the eye of racing stewards looking to nab him for any impropriety — perceived or actual.

In October 1926, he was riding the 9/4 favourite, Myrangle King, at Gosford. During the race, the horse inexplicably dived across towards the fence. Johnstone gathered him up and pulled him away from the fence. The horse finished well but was beaten by two lengths. The stewards had no doubts that Johnstone was up to no good and, despite the intervention of both the trainer and owner on his behalf, the stewards handed out a demoralising two-year disqualification.

Johnstone was incensed at the treatment meted out to him, and protested his innocence. Incredibly, without an appeal even being heard, he was reinstated after just three months on the sideline and it did not take him long to regain his place among the very top riders. After only four months of the 1927 season, he led the Sydney premiership with an enviable record of 16 wins, five seconds, seven thirds and 33 unplaced mounts.

However, just as he was again seemingly on the point of realising his undoubted talent, Johnstone again fell to the enthusiastic intervention of stewards at the Armidale Cup carnival in 1927.

It was not uncommon to see the top riders of the time attending the lucrative country cup meeting circuit. Top jockeys such as Jim Pike, Ted Bartle, Stan Davidson, Billy Cook and the Munro brothers were much sought after when they attended these big cup carnivals. Johnstone was no different, and he attended the Armidale Cup carnival as the leading Sydney rider.

Johnstone was riding Our Rep in the Flying Handicap. He won the start, but beaten for pace was unable to hold his position with the speedy Saliden and Bright Lad heading him into the turn. The first turn at Armidale was extremely sharp and Our Rep ran wide. Later at the stewards' inquiry, Johnstone emphatically denied that his mount ran right across to the outside fence. He pointed out that if this had been the case, surely Benzol who was behind him would have also headed Our Rep. When Johnstone got Our Rep back to the fence he was still well clear of Benzol. In knowing that his mount had to carry 9 stone 9 pounds [57 kilograms], he patiently sat in behind the leaders. At the home turn, Johnstone was on top of the leaders and shot his mount between them entering the straight. He thrashed Our Rep to the front 50 yards from home and looked like winning until Stan Davidson came with a late run on Benzol and beat him on the post by a head.

Johnstone was thought to have rigged the race. At the stewards' inquiry, both owners and trainer were able to prove that they had backed their horse. The trainer also declared that he felt that Our Rep had run the worst race of its career despite the fact that, when ridden by Johnstone on the first day of the carnival, Our Rep had been well beaten by Saliden by over three and a half lengths. The trainer also said that he had told Johnstone that if he was unable to get to the front then he was to sit in behind the leaders — just the option that the rider had in fact adopted. The most startling evidence revealed at the inquiry was again from the trainer, Moore, who stated that he was suspicious of Johnstone's handling of the horse on the first day. Yet he had again given Johnstone the mount. The stewards called for the bookmaker's books, but nothing suspicious was revealed with regard to Our Rep. It is hard to believe that Johnstone was not riding to win.

Nonetheless, Johnstone was again expelled for two years. And it may not have been his efforts on the track that gave him his suspension. Although riding to win,

Johnstone's behaviour at the inquiry did not match his track behaviour. Apparently, in his usual tempestuous manner, Johnstone had taken offence at the stewards' insinuations during the inquiry. Losing his temper, he upended the stewards' table. It may have been this incident that prompted the stewards to react as they did. No love was lost between Johnstone and the racing hierarchy, and his brash manner was in many instances responsible for getting him into trouble.

Two years out of the spotlight is a long time. Altogether, with his earlier misdemeanours, Johnstone had been barred from riding in Sydney for some four and a half years.

Johnstone returned to race riding in Sydney in 1931. During that season, he won the AJC Oaks on Tantrum. This result put him straight back to the upper echelon of the riding ranks, and he sat in second place on the Sydney Jockeys' Premiership behind Jim Pike.

Johnstone was now separated from his wife, and his reputation as a gambling playboy was well entrenched. He received an unexpected offer to ride for Australian trainer Alec Higgins in India. After years of frustration and faltering ambitions, Johnstone jumped at the chance to chase new riches and prizes abroad. He was very successful in India, and won India's richest race, the Bombay Eclipse. After this victory, he was asked by the racing manager for Sir Victor Sassoon to consider coming to England for Sassoon's team as second stable rider behind jockey Steve Donoghue.

Johnstone arrived in England fit and ready to take up his position. However, he received a severe setback and was clearly angered when the British racing authorities refused to grant him a licence. No reason was given for the refusal, and no clear understanding has since surfaced. Johnstone thought it was because of his misdemeanours back home and his high-rolling playboy image.

But the decision not to grant Johnstone a licence to ride in England does raise some questions. Why were both Johnstone and later Darby Munro singled out for this treatment? Other Australian riders with long suspensions and misdemeanours were able to procure licences to ride. Perhaps it may have had something to do with their apparently 'swarthy' appearance.

Johnstone accompanied Steve Donoghue to France, where he watched the British rider in action from the private box of wealthy French owner Monsieur Pierre Wertheimer. He was offered and accepted an offer to ride for Wertheimer and his brother Paul in France.

Initially, the French criticised Johnstone for his riding style. It was typically Australian and inspired by no particular school. He bent over the neck of his mount and straightened at the finish. He used the whip to strike the neck and top of the shoulder, brushing the hair the wrong way, while his highly active legs

RAE 'TOGO' JOHNSTONE.
COURTESY NEWSPIX.

hammered at the flanks of the horse and forced it to spurt. The effort was short and very violent, and it produced sensational finishes. Eventually the French came to idolise Johnstone, nicknaming him 'Le Crocodile' for his habit of coming from behind with late runs and gobbling up the field to win races on the post.

Much to Johnstone's disgust, he was to be suspended yet again soon after arriving in France. After he won a race at Deauville, the crowd had abused him by pelting him and his mount with stones. The disgruntled punters thought he had roughed up his jockey opponents during the running of the race. The stewards agreed with the punters, and relegated Johnstone's mount to third place and suspended him for 10 days.

The suspension proved to be a blessing in disguise. In France, Johnstone had continued with his high life and gambling habits, and to soothe the wounds of his suspension he took himself to the casino. Here he met the beautiful former Follies Bergere showgirl Marie Gui, who had an immediate calming impact on him: he gave up his gambling and playboy life.

Johnstone did not take long to be successful in France. Only two years after leaving Australia, he won the 1933 French Jockeys' Premiership. He went on to take the title three times in his first six seasons in France. He also learnt to speak French so fluently that apparently some French owners had to be reminded that he was indeed Australian. Through gaining a French jockey's licence, Johnstone had sidestepped the British racing authorities. He was now able to ride in Britain no matter what they thought of him. He rode his first major European winners when he took out both the English One Thousand and Two Thousand Guineas. However, Johnstone's first ride in the historic English Derby of 1933 was a disaster. He came in 12th behind the legendary Hyperion, and it was the beginning of a love/hate relationship between Johnstone and the premier race.

In 1934, he was retained by Lord Glanely, the owner of the biggest racing stables in Britain. Johnstone had already won the Two Thousand Guineas on Glanely's colt Colombo. The ease of this victory had seen him installed as a firm favourite for the English Derby. But Johnstone was the target of an unscrupulous attempt to derail the chances of Colombo in the Derby when he was offered the incredible sum of £10,000 to ensure that the favourite lost. He declared that 'moral considerations apart, there was no temptation whatever'. However, Johnstone did not ride one of his best tactical races in the Derby. He was cluttered up on the fence rounding Tattenham Corner. Finally forcing his way out, Colombo came with a sizzling late rush but could not overhaul the winner, Windsor Lad, and the runner-up, Easton. Johnstone was publicly crucified over his ride, and it haunted him for years. In a repeat performance the very next year, Johnstone suffered a similar experience, this time with a French-trained filly, Mesa. Having won the One Thousand Guineas, the partnership started favourite for the Oaks. In a slowly run muddling race, Johnstone got himself hopelessly boxed in on the rails, extricating himself when the race was all over to finish a flying third.

Johnstone journeyed back across the channel to France, deeply bitter over these defeats and his treatment at the hands of the press and public. He gained some consolation as he won the 1933 Prix du Conseil Municipal and the 1934 Grand Prix de Saint Cloud on Aussureus.

As war grew imminent, Johnstone's career went into hiatus. First he was rejected by France for military service and, with the sudden capitulation of the French in the face of Hitler's blitzkrieg, Johnstone and wife Marie abandoned their Paris apartment and fled to Spain ahead of the advancing Nazi forces. On being refused visas, they set up house in the south of France and obviously hoped to see out the war in relative safely. But the pressures of war and dwindling assets forced them to flee again, this time to the presumed safety of Monte Carlo — assumed to be neutral territory. Johnstone was granted permission to travel each weekend to race meetings at centres such as Lyon, Vichy and Marseilles.

The meeting on 8 November 1942 in Marseilles proved to be one of personal success but may have resulted in compromising both his and his wife's safety. News had spread rapidly across the course that the Allies had landed successfully in North Africa. The crowd identified the Australian rider with the heroic 'Diggers' fighting in North Africa, and they reserved all their support and cheering for Johnstone's mounts. Their vociferous approval increased as he proceeded to win two events. These events may have triggered Johnstone's arrest two months later by Italian security officers when he was removed with other foreigners to a detention centre in the Maritime Alps. The barracks were grim, and he was held for some six months. He was eventually allowed to stay with Marie in confinement in a small hotel where they remained until the Italian Army surrendered and they were able to return to Nice.

Any thoughts of safety in Nice were quickly dispelled. German troops were everywhere. Johnstone's only form of identification was his French licence, and incredibly this satisfied inspection on several occasions. The couple decided that Monte Carlo was a much safer haven, and they made their way back to the principality. Johnstone knew his good luck was running short and when the Gestapo eventually came knocking on the door of the apartment he and Marie shared in November 1943, he had a bag already packed.

Marie tried to follow him, but was pushed back as Johnstone was hauled off to a prison camp in the Vosges Mountains, 600 kilometres north of Monte

Carlo. The food was inedible and Johnstone and other inmates threw it away and survived on the weekly Red Cross parcels. Eight months later, the Allies landed at Normandy and orders were given for the camp prisoners to be moved from France to Germany. Johnstone was given a lucky break. The French resistance blew up the railway lines en route to Germany, forcing the train to halt at the town of Belfort. Marie and other wives, learning of this, arrived at the station to say goodbye to their husbands. Johnstone grabbed a bucket and dropped to the platform, as if to follow a couple of fellow prisoners who had been allowed to go for water, but instead he turned in the opposite direction and walked towards Marie and the crowd of women. His mouth was dry and he expected a bullet in the back at any moment, but he kept going and, undetected, walked into the crowd of women. He and Marie simply slipped away.

The mother of a resistance fighter allowed Johnstone to hide in an attic for three months until, dressed as a peasant in beret and tattered clothes, he and Marie joined a resistance group. They endured a difficult journey trudging through snow and heavily mined fields, past German lines and to a liberated Paris.

Shortly after the end of the war, Johnstone signed up as the number one jockey for the French cotton magnate Marcel de Boussac, and over the next decade plundered dozens of big English race meetings on his horses. Bookmakers watched for de Boussac's aircraft landing on the centre of the British courses. If Johnstone was in the party, they knew big business was at hand. The de Boussac team was formidable and included trainer Henri Semblat, racing manager Comte de Brignac and jockey Rae Johnstone. De Boussac was in racing for business, not fun, and each of his 200 horses in training was carefully watched for profits. The de Boussac stable was reported to have made more than £250,000 a year from racing. His mares and stallions at his breeding establishment on the southern tip of the Falaise Gap were valued at more than £3 million.

Johnstone did not miss winning any race of importance in France. He took the Prix du Conseil Municipal in 1933 on Aussureus, in 1946 on Vandale, in 1948 on Espace Vital and in 1952 on Worden. He also won the 1934 Grand Prix de Saint Cloud on Assureus. He won the prestigious Prix de l'Arc de Triomph in 1945 on Nikellora and again in 1954 on Sica Boy. In 1945 he won the Grand Prix de la Ville Vichy on Achille. He twice won the Grand Prix de Deauville, one of his favourite courses: in 1948 on Turmoil and in 1955 on Rose Bonheur. The Prix de Diane at Chantilly fell to him in 1947 on Montenica and the Prix de Jockey Club on the same course in 1948 on Bey and in 1952 on Auriban.

For Johnstone, 1947 was a bumper year. He won the Arc de Triomph on Nikellora and marked his return to riding in Britain by finally breaking through, making it third time lucky winning the One Thousand Guineas and Oaks on Impudence. But it proved only a prelude to what would be his greatest ever season.

In 1948, Johnstone finally overcame his hoodoo in the English Derby, becoming the first Australian jockey to win what is arguably racing's greatest prize. Johnstone sent a telegram to the Press Club Derby Luncheon. It read: 'Bon Apetit, My Love to all.' Two days later, Johnstone and My Love erased the memory of his first disastrous Derby 14 years earlier.

My Love was a heavily built, short-legged colt with a bold eye. Johnstone could not wait to partner him. My Love was trained and had won in France and Johnstone persuaded the Aga Khan to buy a half-share.

Johnstone's ride in the Derby was impeccable. Rounding Tattenham Corner for the run up the home straight, My Love still had half the field in front of him but Johnstone produced a miracle rails run. Stablemate Royal Drake had hit the front and looked the winner when Johnstone burst through on My Love. He passed Royal Drake a hundred metres from the post and won running away. Johnstone declared it to be his 'happiest ever sensation aboard a horse'. He sent the winning Jockey's Cup back to his mother in Australia.

The victory on My Love was to trigger one of the most incredible runs of success ever achieved at the highest levels of racing. Johnstone won the Prix du Jockey Club at Chantilly on Bey eight days after the Derby. Two days later, at Royal Ascot, he notched up a fabulous treble: the Royal Hunt Cup on Master Vote, the King Edward VII Stakes on Vic Day and the Queen Alexandra Stakes on Vulgan. He took out his first Irish Derby on Nathoo and four days after that, steered My Love home again to win the Grand Prix du Paris at Longchamps. For good measure, he also won the 1948 French Derby, completing a hat-trick of Derby successes that no one else has repeated. The victory of Nathoo in the Irish Derby was, significantly, the ace Australian rider's first mount in the Emerald Isle. Strong, stylish in his own inimitable way and possessing the temperament of a great big-race rider, as his record shows, Rae Johnstone must rank among the greatest jockeys to grace the roll of honour of the Irish Derby.

Johnstone again won the English Derby in 1950. This ride on Galcador was possibly his greatest.

 *Although Galcador was only a mile horse, Johnstone took him to the front coming round Tattenham Corner, thereby catching his rival jockeys napping. He kept Galcador going to the post when he should have been spent. Galcador had started at 100/9. Johnstone was 51 when he rode his third English Derby winner. Lavendin was a genuine stayer who started 7/1 favourite in 1956 and found the mile and a half no trouble with Johnstone in the saddle.*

Johnstone's run of success in these years may have been directly related to the post-war dominance of French horses. As their supremacy began to wane, so too did his fortunes, although the classic successes of Talma II in the St Leger, Sun Cap in the Oaks and Lavendin in the Derby enabled him to relish his altered reputation in England for several more years.

It was in England that Johnstone enjoyed his swan song in the saddle on what he regarded as his favourite horse: Hugh Lupus. Although robbed by injury from the Epsom Derby, Hugh Lupus made amends as a 4-year-old. Ridden each time by Johnstone, he won the March Stakes, Hardwicke Stakes, Scarborough Stakes and Champion Stakes.

After 3000 winners, Rae Johnstone retired from the saddle in 1957, bowing out at Longchamps, the scene of so many spectacular, come-from-behind triumphs for this unorthodox but supremely effective jockey. He then began training in France but without much success. A rumoured riding comeback never materialised, and he died suddenly following a heart attack in Paris in 1964.

For the last 20 years of his life, Johnstone dined only at the finest restaurants and was recognised as a man with a sophisticated palate and a profound knowledge of food and wine. During the 1950s, he was probably the highest paid sportsman in Europe. He went to only the best tailors in Paris and London and wore shirts of the finest silks and handcrafted shoes. In the saddle, he was daring and crafty, able to spot an opening before his rivals and to show a masterly judge of pace.

His unrivalled list of big race victories during the last decade of his career was an unprecedented avalanche of major victories, and stands as a testament to his skill and competitive nature.

LIFTING THE MYSTERY?

As with Peter St Albans, mystery surrounds Rae Johnstone's background. Almost inevitably, given the condemnation of the era, Johnston may have decided to pass himself off as being from a Portuguese background. At the time, he said his real name was Davies and that he had been forced to take his grandmother's maiden name, Johnstone, when he became apprenticed because there were several other jockeys named Davies at the time. However, Rae Johnstone was born at New Lambton, a suburb of Newcastle, in 1905. His father was Robert J Johnstone and his mother was Elizabeth. Robert was born at Lambton in 1884. Rae Johnstone's grandmother was Olivia Johnstone, but most interestingly his grandfather was listed as unknown. There is no mention of the name Davies or any Portuguese links, and the fact that his grandfather was recorded as 'unknown' further adds to the story of Johnstone's Aboriginal heritage. It was a fairly common practice to write Aboriginal parentage out of official documentation.

At the peak of his career in Europe, Johnstone could not be persuaded to talk about his origins in Sydney, and apart from seeing his mother he was never keen to get back to his home city. The doyen of Australian sports writing, Jack Pollard, recalled that 'it was as though there was something there he wanted to forget'. Even more conclusive is the fact that an Aboriginal, man Bruce Kendall, contacted the author, revealing that Johnstone was in fact his relative! The Kendalls originated from the Cobar area of western New South Wales. Kendall revealed:

> Togo Johnstone would have been my grandmother's uncle … Granny Wilson was a Johnstone and this branch of the family by coincidence consisted of all horse people. There were other jockeys in the family too, bush jockeys. Although apparently one of them way back went to Melbourne to be apprenticed as a jockey.

Kendall was adamant that Rae Johnstone, like many other Aboriginal people of this particular period, was left with no alternative other than to hide his Aboriginality.

DAVID HUGH 'DARBY' MUNRO

Taking off the blinkers

TRIUMPHS

Melbourne Cup
AJC Derby
VRC Derby
AJC Epsom
AJC Sires Produce Stakes
VRC St Leger
Doncaster
Champagne Stakes

DARBY MUNRO IN THE SADDLE ON PETER PAN., C.1930S. COURTESY NEWSPIX.

By rights Darby Munro should not be included in a book about Aboriginal jockeys, as he is not Aboriginal. This is quite clear from the documentation held by his family's descendants. Yet, in my original study, several prominent Aboriginal riders such as Darby McCarthy, Merv Maynard, William Lord and Gordon Taylor were convinced in interviews that Munro was Aboriginal. Why did these men who rode against Munro and shared the jockeys' room with him become so convinced he was Aboriginal? Throughout his career, Munro claimed a Jewish background, and he was often labelled as swarthy in the press. When my first book came out, noted racing journalist Bill Casey declared firmly that 'the truth is his own background was Jewish'. Conversations with descendants of the Munro family can conclusively and with 100 per cent authority dismiss any claim of Jewish ancestry in the family. The Munro family is Catholic! Genealogical evidence uncovered by the family reveals that they are unlikely to have any Aboriginal connection, 'which would come from way out of left field'.

I decided to keep Darby Munro in this book because of his connection with and inspiration to so many Aboriginal riders. Forty-five years after his death, Darby Munro is still regarded by many as the greatest jockey Australia has produced. He and his brother Jim — another of the greatest Australian jockeys — moved with their family from Melbourne to Sydney when they were young. On horseback they were both child prodigies and schoolboy stars of the impromptu races on Payten's Paddock, against ponies ridden by Cyril Angles, Rae Johnstone, Mick Heynes and other boys from the Randwick area. In 1923, the leviathan Melbourne punter Eric Connelly was so impressed by the manner in which the then 10-year-old Darby handled horses in track gallops for his father, Hugh Munro, that he took Darby to Melbourne to help train his string of 50 horses. They included champions such as Manfred, Rampion, Pantheon and Bicolor. Although he could not ride in races until he was 14, young Darby had a close-up look at luxurious living in a year when Connelly took more than £100,000 from the betting ring and won successive Newmarket Handicaps with Rostrum in 1922 and Sunburst in 1923.

He established a great record in Australia's greatest races. He won three Melbourne Cups, on Peter Pan in 1934, Sirius in 1944 and Russia in 1946. He captured the AJC Derby five times, the VRC Derby five times, the AJC Epsom twice, the AJC Sires Produce Stakes four times, the VRC St Leger four times, the Doncaster twice and the Champagne Stakes four times.

Punters were not kind to Munro. A love–hate relationship persisted between the great rider and the punters who periodically lined the fence to heckle him with racist abuse when he was beaten.

'You black bastard.'

'You black bludger.'

Munro never lost the taste for high living.

> No one would have mistaken swarthy-visaged dapper David Hugh Munro (Darby to you) for anything but a rich jockey. Even if his 5 feet 2 inches [157.5 centimetres] and slight figure were not signal lights, he had the slight swagger of the racecourse, the talk of the racecourse and frequently the companions of the racecourse. Because racing is one of Australia's mental narcotics, because ability to ride a horse and win a horse race seems more important and brings greater reward than scholarly attainment, Munro was a public figure. The crowd stopped to stare when he alighted from his car. Police officers have been seen to give him precedence in traffic; men, who are his superiors in everything but racing lore, hung on his words. Not that Munro himself chased the limelight. He made

> no display of his wealth. He lived with his wife and two children (he has been married twice), in a modest flat overlooking Randwick racecourse. He did not throw his money about to claim attention. But he was seldom out of the news. Darby Munro was one of the sporting paradoxes of the years. The public hated him — and loved him wildly. What there was in his personality which made racegoers both hot and cold no psychiatrist could diagnose.
>
> — *Sporting Life, December 1948*

Despite Munro's highly successful career, he had to struggle with racing officialdom, including a possibly unjust two-year suspension for a ride on Vagabond in Melbourne. The family was clannish and Jim and Darby's mother doted on them, berating anyone who suggested that they had ridden a poor race. Their sister kept a photographic record of their careers as Jockeys on the walls of her home.

Jibes and innuendo targeting Munro's background are obvious from his various nicknames. Famous trainer Dick Wootton labelled him as 'shover', but he was also known as the 'Brown Bomber', the 'Coon' and the 'Demon': the Brown Bomber because he hit a horse with the same power as a Joe Lois punch; the Coon because of his dark complexion; the Demon because he could be a fury on a horse in a close finish.

Certainly, after he had given up riding and trained a small team of horses at Randwick, Darby Munro came into contact with and pursued a number of younger Aboriginal riders. He tried to procure Gordon Taylor's indentures from Keith Tinson. He gave Jimmy Leslie rides on his horses. He was also a contact and long-time friend of Rae Johnstone. Darby McCarthy gained the name Darby in reverence to the great man, and often stayed with Munro at his Coogee Bay Hotel towards the end of Munro's life. Darby McCarthy stated that Munro had even confided to him that he was Aboriginal. Why did Munro do this? I can't believe that Munro was just pulling McCarthy's leg. It is quite possible that Munro had empathy with Aboriginal people — certainly the racial abuse to which he was often subjected gave him some sort of inside knowledge of what it meant to be Aboriginal.

For what it is worth, there remain some interesting links. The Munro name is a well-known Aboriginal family name. Darby Munro's father, Hugh, was a famed horseman, who trained Revenue to win the Melbourne Cup in 1901. Hugh Munro prepared Revenue at none other than St Albans' Stud. In late 1876, when Hugh Munro was employed by James Wilson at St Albans' Stud, he was riding on the training grounds in company with another boy who was mounted on a high-spirited animal. His companion's animal took fright and threw up his hind feet, one of them striking Munro on the leg. The animal fortunately was without shoes, but nevertheless the boy was seriously injured and was taken to hospital for treatment.

Twenty-two years later, Hugh Munro was still very much a part of the St Albans' inner sanctum. Among the many large floral tributes at the funeral of Peter St Albans was one supplied by Mr and Mrs Hugh Munro. Obviously close to St Albans, Hugh Munro also acted as a pallbearer alongside James Wilson Snr. This connection may well have been just a coincidence, but could Peter St Albans and Hugh Munro have been related or did they just both work for Wilson at St Albans' Stud and strike up a friendship? This evidence offers a previously unknown link between the Munro family and Peter St Albans.

In conclusion, as stated family documentation reveals, Munro could not possibly be Aboriginal without some totally unknown and unexpected twist. The evidence of the Aboriginal jockeys who were adamant that Darby Munro was Aboriginal was most probably influenced by the fact that they could relate to the racial taunts to which Munro was subjected, or recognise his generosity and concerns that made them believe he was Aboriginal. The revelations to Darby McCarthy will remain a complete mystery.

One interesting connection between Darby Munro and Rae Johnstone that has not been analysed before is that they were both refused licences to ride by the British racing authorities. It was claimed that the refusal was because of their record of falling foul of officialdom and suspensions. This argument hardly holds up with the fact that George Moore served a two-and-a-half-year suspension from riding in the mid-1950s and had no trouble in procuring a clearance to ride in Britain; similarly, no rider carried greater stain or insinuation on his character than Athol George Mulley over his handling of Bernborough in the 1946 Caulfield Cup, yet Mulley was also cleared to ride in Britain. In the largely all-white domain of British horse racing at that time, could the refusal to Munro and Johnstone have had anything to do with their often-described 'swarthy' looks?

Mr A. I. Maple-Brown's blk. g. "ALINGA" Jockey M. Maynard.
Tetreen — Ray's Ornament
Trainer P. Graham.

MERV MAYNARD

The sport of kings

TRIUMPHS
More than 1500 winners
Sydney Turf Club Cup
Queen's Cup
Australian Jockey Club Shorts Handicap
Australian Jockey Club Cannonbury Stakes
Queensland Turf Club Lightning Handicap
Newcastle Cup
Newcastle Newmarket
Grafton Cup
Whangarei Cup (New Zealand)
Penang Cup (Malaysia)
Sultans Cup (Singapore)

On 22 February 1992, 40 years after he won the Queen's Cup, Merv Maynard shook hands with Queen Elizabeth II and chatted for 40 minutes. It was a huge step away from the boy who began his working life washing bottles in a Lakemba chemist shop.

Times were extremely difficult for his family during Maynard's youth. His father was a high profiled Aboriginal political activist harassed by the police. Following a so-called accident on the wharf, Fred Maynard was severely injured and was unable to work and provide for his family of seven, who survived on £3 a fortnight and handouts from the St Vincent de Paul.

Fred Maynard was a very outspoken man in a dangerous time. He fought for Aboriginal rights to land, protecting Aboriginal kids being taken from their families by the government and defending a distinct Aboriginal cultural identity. There was no inquiry or investigation into the 'so-called' accident. It was all just hushed up. At the time, the police were not above frightening the families of Aboriginal activists. Merv Maynard himself recalled as a young boy of 5 or 6 being picked up by the police with another young Aboriginal boy, and being taken to Canterbury police station. At the station, the young boys were frightened out of their wits by the police. My father stated that it was the most terrifying moment of his life. When one considers his years as a jockey and the serious falls he encountered, to say that this moment at the police station was the most frightening of his life bears some reflection. When he was finally released, he ran home and hid in his room, not uttering a word to either his mother or father.

In recent years, he has reflected on this moment, and has theorised that the police were sending a threatening message through to his father to stop his political agitation. The message was clear: 'We can pick up your kids anytime we like!' But of course my father in this instance never said a word — he thought he might be in more trouble, so he just clammed up.

After his father's death, Merv Maynard spent a lot of time with various uncles and aunts. He first worked in a chemist shop and then took a job as a delivery boy for the local post office: it looked as if the diminutive Maynard was in for a life of lumping mailbags. However, on visits to his aunts and uncles in Newcastle, he began to haunt the Broadmeadow racecourse, where he came under the notice of leading trainer Keith Tinson. This was hardly surprising. With a weight of just 4 stone 5 pounds (27.7 kilograms), young Maynard looked to be a natural jockey.

But things appeared bleak on the racing front when young Maynard had to return to his mother's Lakemba home. He was not to be denied, however, and spent much of his spare time with his face pressed against the tin fence of Canterbury racecourse, watching the trainers and stablehands at early morning track gallops and race meetings.

One day he recognised a familiar face. Keith Tinson had brought a couple of horses down to race at Canterbury. Maynard called out to the trainer through a hole in the fence, and Tinson obliged by asking attendants to let him on to the course where he spent the day tending Tinson's horses. Impressed by the boy's keenness and energy, Tinson offered him an apprenticeship as a jockey. With his mother's approval, Maynard journeyed back to Newcastle with Tinson to begin his life in racing.

Stable life was very hard back in the late 1940s. It was not until he was a full 12 months into his apprenticeship that Maynard was even allowed the time to attend a movie. He lived in a little room at the back of the stables. It was very rough and crude, but Mrs Howe, who looked after some of the young jockeys, put up curtains trying to make it into a home for him. Maynard had no money – maybe a pound a week at the most. He was withdrawn, quiet and shy, keeping to himself as an apprentice. He was just a boy from Lakemba, from the wrong side of the tracks. He had no father and was out in the hard wide world of knocks — and he took them.

MERV MAYNARD AGED 14. COURTESY MAYNARD FAMILY COLLECTION.

MERV MAYNARD, AS AN 18-YEAR-OLD APPRENTICE, PACKING FOR THE 1951 CAULFIELD CUP.

Maynard could not have picked a more successful stable to join. In his first season (1948–49), he rode eight winners and quickly came to the notice of other trainers. The next season he rode 10 winners, including one in the Quirindi Cup.

His first success was at Wyong on 16 April 1949, when he won on Paragon. When Maynard had to go for his first race, and he had no suitable clothes, shoes or hat to wear, Mrs Howe sorted out a pair of tan and white golf shoes — fashionable at the time for women — that fitted him. The sprigs were knocked off and from that day on they were his shoes. He needed a hat because jockeys had to look very conservative and neat, so they put Mr Howe's hat on him and sent him off to the races.

Stable life was regimental, and Tinson ruled the stables with a very strict hand. The apprentice jockeys used to ride early morning trackwork, then they would have to come back and muck out the stables, sweeping out everything and all around the yard, and cleaning all the sandrolls. Lunch was a sandwich or something similar. They were not able to go home for lunch or sit up at a table with a good meal as the trainers did.

Old Roy James had a major influence on Maynard's riding. James had been a top rider during a long career, but by this time he was more or less a trackwork rider. James was a riding grandfather when Maynard's career began, and he was tragically killed in a trackwork fall at Canterbury years later. Stan Davidson was another jockey who influenced Maynard, although he hung up his saddle just after Maynard started riding. Hickey, Thompson and Waterson were also all great local riders of the period. Neil Waterson in particular was a very good jockey, an intelligent rider, pretty to watch, neat and polished in the saddle and a thorough professional. To Maynard, they were all great horsemen — an attribute he feels many of today's jockeys lack.

The 1950–51 season was to see Merv Maynard propelled into national racing prominence. He rode Warrah King to victory in the AJC Shorts handicap at Randwick and also the QTC Lightning Handicap at Eagle farm in Brisbane. In the Lightning, Warrah King whipped a smart field winning by three lengths. The victory in the Lightning elevated Warrah King to favouritism for the Doomben Ten Thousand. If Warrah King had won the Ten Thousand ridden by an 18-year-old apprentice, it would have given the youthful Maynard's career an enormous boost. Sadly, however, it was not to be.

George Moore riding on his outside shouted: 'Let him go son, let him go, it's your race.' 'Not yet, not yet,' Maynard replied. Third on the home turn and hooked out on straightening they look the winner, when suddenly Warrah King receives a severe check from eventual winner Coniston. They crash heavily to the turf and Maynard has 26 horses go over and past him. Miraculously, the young jockey walks away from the fall with nothing more than a broken big toe and a broken dream.

Another disappointment occurred in September 1951. At Randwick, before a crowd of 68,000, Maynard rode the 100/1 Queensland outsider Rinkeno in the AJC Epsom Handicap. Hugging the fence all the way, Rinkeno split through an opening and stormed home late, failing to catch the winner Davey Jones by the barest of margins going down in a photo finish.

These disappointments were not important, however. Young Maynard had come to the notice of many of the big-time trainers, who now clamoured for the young Newcastle rider hailed as the 'Darby Munro of the Bush' and 'Tinson's Goldmine'. It was not until Wayne Harris appeared on the racing scene in the late 1970s that another northern apprentice became so sought after by the big stables to ride in the major feature races of the Australian racing calendar. This was despite the fact that Newcastle apprentices during those intervening years included top jockeys as good as John Wade and Robert Thompson.

Before he was 21, Maynard had ridden in three successive Caulfield Cups (1951, 1952 and 1953), in Epsoms, Metropolitans, Doncasters, Doomben Ten Thousands, Doomben Cups and the LKS Mackinnon Stakes, and had the chance to ride in the Melbourne Cup.

The Melbourne Cup of 1952 was the year of the sensational Dalray, which justly won the event. Maynard's great thrill was to pilot 3-year-old Ocean Spray for leading Sydney trainer Danny Lewis into eleventh place behind the New Zealand champion, Dalray. Ocean Spray had been well supported in the event, and was backed to win over £50,000 in the Flemington two-miler.

The same year also saw Maynard achieve a victory that was to have repercussions some 41 years later. He rode Sydney trainer Norman Dewsbury's horse Salamanca in the first Queen's Cup at Randwick on 11 October 1952. The Queen's Cup in 1952 was regarded as nothing more than a two-horse race between two champions of the period: Hydrogen and Dalray. Other runners were considered to be merely in there to make up the numbers. Maynard had different ideas, however.

As Maynard approaches the long Randwick straight he lets loose on Salamanca racing to the front, a tough seasoned stayer carrying the featherweight of 7st 2lb [45.5 kilograms]. Jockeys [Keith Nuttall and Darby Munro] on the two champions have been playing a cat and mouse game with each other and have been caught by surprise. Salamanca quickly takes the lead from Headstockman and sets sail for the post, leaving the others with far too much to do. Dalray has made up a lot of ground late but Maynard has pinched the race on the turn.

The young rider proudly received the accolades of the crowd at the presentation made by the Governor-General. His only disappointment was that, if the King had not died, he would have met the then Princess Elizabeth.

MERV MAYNARD AND NORMAN DEWSBURY AT RANDWICK AFTER SALAMANCA'S WIN IN THE FIRST QUEEN'S CUP IN 1952. COURTESY MAYNARD FAMILY COLLECTION.

Maynard was now firmly established among the elite riders in Australia, riding for trainers TJ Smith, Danny Lewis, Harry Plant and Vic Thompson. He also rode for high-profile owners such as flamboyant restaurateur Azzalin 'the Dazzlin' Romano and newspaper magnate Sir Frank Packer — the only person who intimidated him with a sense of power.

Maynard's first meeting with Sir Frank Packer occurred when Maynard was only 20. He received a call in Newcastle saying that Packer wanted him to ride his horse, Top Level, in the 1953 Caulfield Cup, and that he wanted him to come to his Sydney office for a meeting. Maynard was still a shy young man, and on arriving at the *Daily Telegraph* office building in Sydney he did not enter through the front but went to the back where the newspapers were being loaded on to trucks.

'How do I get to Mr Frank Packer's office?' he asked one of the workmen.

The workmen looked Maynard up and down and then pointed to a lift and replied:

> 'See that lift over there, boy? Well get in that and when it gets to the top that's Frank's office.'

Maynard followed the instructions and on alighting found himself in what he describes as the biggest office imaginable, with a great shining table endlessly stretching into the distance, only stopped at the other end by the imposing figure of the seated Frank Packer. As Frank sat at one end of the table booming out his instructions on how he wanted his horse ridden, the only part of Merv Maynard that was visible was the top of his head from his eyes up. Even with all Sir Frank's expert tips and instructions, Top Level still ran unplaced in Caulfield Cup.

It was around this time that Maynard received the first of many lucrative offers to move away from Newcastle. The offer from the Chinese multi-millionaire movie mogul brothers Run Run and Run Me Shaw was one that Maynard jumped at. They wanted young Maynard to be their stable jockey in Singapore and Malaysia, and he readily accepted. He was devastated when his former boss, Keith Tinson, complained to the Australian Jockey Club and took steps to prevent him from accepting the position. Maynard was out of his apprenticeship, but because he was not yet 21 years of age, they deemed that technically he was still under the control of Tinson. Maynard still has the letter that the Australian Jockey Club sent him, stating that if he attempted to take the position with the Shaw brothers, the club would not issue him with a jockey's licence and that he would not be able to ride.

Top jockey Athol George Mulley subsequently gained the position when Maynard reluctantly turned down the offer. Mulley spent three seasons in the East as the leading rider in a very lucrative environment. Maynard, hiding his disappointment, continued successfully on the home front, winning the AJC Cannonbury Stakes on the Vic Thompson-trained Gulf Palm.

On many occasions during the 46 years that Maynard rode, he received enthusiastic calls from many different trainers asking him to ride one of their horses. Many confided that they had unearthed a champion! Maynard received such a call one late night in early May 1953 from a little-known young southern district trainer, Paul Graham.

The horse was Alinga, a jet-black gelding by Tetreen out of Ray's Ornament. He was bred and raced by Mr AJ Maple Brown, a wealthy grazier from the Goulburn district. Ray's Ornament was ridden by his owner in the Light Horse Brigade.

Maynard had heard countless trainers echo the words, 'I want you to ride a champion.' Most were disappointments. However, he looks back with relish to that May day in 1953 when he was in the enclosure receiving his riding instructions from Paul Graham. This was the only time during his career that Maynard experienced the hairs on his neck literally stand on end just from the look of a horse. He would never forget that first view of Alinga striding into the enclosure. He was a magnificent animal — a giant, jet-black gelding who fairly rippled with muscle and power.

'If your horse can gallop anything like he looks then you might have a champion,' Maynard confided to Graham.

Alinga's city debut was in the 11 furlong (2200 metre) Campsie Graduation at Canterbury. Under the set weight conditions of the event, Alinga carried what for him must have seemed like a postage stamp of 8 stone 8 pounds (54.4 kilograms). The bush champ was elevated to 3/1 second elect in the betting markets for the event, behind even-money favourite Audacious, ridden by Jack Thompson. It was nothing more than an exercise gallop for Alinga, which cruised to the post, winning by one and a half lengths.

Sydney racing experts were unanimous in their praise, hailing Alinga as the best horse to come out of the country in years. But the initial gloss was tarnished with Alinga's next three runs. He was beaten by Prince Dakhil in a photo finish in the 11 furlong (2200 metre) May Handicap at Warwick Farm. Then the unthinkable happened: he ran unplaced for the first time in his career in the 10 furlong (2000 metre) Tattersalls James Barnes Plate at Randwick, with the winner again being Prince Dakhil. Nine days later, Alinga was back on the track. This time he was beaten into second place in a photo finish by Royal Glitter in the Coronation Cup at Randwick.

A fortnight later, Alinga was entered at Canterbury in the 9 furlong (1800 metre) Birthday Handicap. Alinga received huge betting support and was backed into 5/2 favourite. Third on the turn, Maynard set Alinga alight and he swept past the leaders as if they were standing still. He eventually eased down on the line, winning by four lengths and clipping a full second from the track record. This win was good enough for Sydney bookmakers to install Alinga as equal favourite with Hydrogen for the upcoming Doomben Cup. But Alinga had no luck in Brisbane after drawing the extreme outside barrier of 26. The bush champ never got on the track, and although second at the leger, he faded in the run to the line. The winner was French Echo, which Alinga had beaten pointlessly at their last meeting in Sydney.

Only five days after his Doomben failure, the 'iron horse' was saddled up for the Grafton Cup, carrying top weight of 9 stone 3 pounds (60.8 kilograms). He was driven to victory by Merv Maynard at his vigorous best, just pipping Britavah, ridden by renowned country jockey Skeeter Kelly, by a half-head. Close-up third was Ben's Hero, ridden by another well-known country rider, Bill Wade. There was still no rest for the hardy Alinga. Fourteen days later, he was back in Sydney where, on 1 August 1953, he contested the Sydney Turf Club Cup at Rosehill. Well-weighted at only 8 stone 6 pounds (53.5 kilograms), Alinga was immediately made favourite for the 12 furlong (2400 metre) event. It was another brilliant ride by Merv Maynard, as he got the favourite home by a length from Athol George Mulley's mount, Lord Saunders. The winner's cheque was £2436, with a gold cup valued at £300.

> Jockey M Maynard always had Alinga in a winning position and left the rails only approaching the home turn where Alinga made his winning run. Alinga jumped smartly in second place behind Ben Bow but when the field moved past the winning post the first time Maynard had settled Alinga down in fifth position behind the leaders Tibridge and Radiant Prince. Alinga was still in that position until the half-mile when Maynard started to move him up a little. Alinga's run carried him quickly up to the leaders and he gained the front when they turned into the straight. Lord Saunders appeared to have a winning chance when Mulley moved him up smartly from seventh position at the turn but as he gained ground Lord Saunders started to run about and hang in.
> — *Sunday Telegraph, 8 February 1953*

> His [Alinga's] success was a tribute to his handling by jockey Mervyn Maynard. Maynard stole a march on the opposition by racing Alinga up sharply approaching the turn. He was in a winning position when the field settled down for the run home. The moment he was clear, Maynard took Alinga over to the rails and his mount finished full of running to hold off the challenge by Lord Saunders.
> — *Sunday Herald, 8 February 1953*

As a result of this victory, Alinga was posted as an early favourite for the Caulfield and Melbourne Cups. He was sent back to Goulburn for a short seven-week let-up, and then returned to Sydney where he was entered in the 7 furlong (1400 metre) Theo Marks Quality Handicap at Rosehill. Alinga was beaten for early pace in the event, but flashed home most impressively to finish fifth behind Carioca. Alinga's final lead-up race for the AJC Metropolitan Handicap was the

10 furlong (2000 metre) Squatters Handicap on the opening day of the 1953 Randwick Carnival. Alinga again received heavy betting support and was backed into 9/4 favourite for the event.

Disaster was to strike, however. Alinga was just making his move at the leaders when suddenly he faltered. When interviewed after the race, Merv Maynard said he felt Alinga stumble soon after straightening.

'I was just going around the leaders when Alinga's leg seemed to go on him,' the jockey said.

It was apparent that the injury was a serious one, and when the horse was led back into the enclosure, his young trainer Paul Graham broke down in tears. The horse was in obvious distress but the initial prognosis was that it was most likely torn ligaments in the rear nearside pastern. Alinga was floated back to his Randwick stables, where it soon became apparent that the injury was far more serious. The horse needed to be physically lifted from the float. Close veterinarian examination revealed that the near fetlock joint had been broken. Thereafter, a 16-day battle was waged and every attempt made to save Alinga's life. Efforts to patch up the shattered leg, including a last-minute appeal by a doctor to allow the horse to recuperate on his property, failed and on 9 October 1953, under the direction of the RSPCA, Alinga was destroyed.

A leading Melbourne trainer brought Maynard once more into the spotlight when, in the hope of securing one of Australia's best lightweight jockeys, he made one of the most fabulous offers of the time for a rider's services in Australia: a retainer of £1000. In addition to this money, Maynard was to receive £25 a week as a living allowance, the use of a car and a percentage of all placed mounts. Although most jockeys — some in even more demand than the Newcastle 'king of the pigskin' — would have rushed to accept, the shy and unassuming Merv Maynard didn't want to leave Newcastle, so he refused the offer.

Alinga's death saw Maynard step away from metropolitan racing for a while, and take to the country cup circuit. Over the next 40 years, he amassed what is most likely the most impressive array of country cup victories ever achieved in New South Wales: the Muswellbrook (3), Cessnock (2), Armidale, Lismore, Tamworth, Grafton, Kembla, Scone, Coffs Harbour, Quirindi, Wellington, Port Macquarie (2), Aberdeen, Denman, Gulgong, Mudgee, Taree, Parkes, Dubbo and Gulargambone Cups, to name only a few that gained a place on the Maynard sideboard. During the 1950s, it was not an uncommon occurrence — especially at his home track of Broadmeadow — to see Maynard riding three or four winners a meeting. He rode five winners at a meeting twice: at Newcastle and Wyong.

In 1958, Maynard was finally tempted away from Newcastle when he accepted an offer to ride in New Zealand for trainer Larry Wiggins. He arrived in New Zealand in time for the New Year's Day Auckland Cup meeting. He rode in the Auckland Cup and had a number of other mounts on the day. In complete contrast to today, with many Kiwi riders riding in Australia, in 1958 many of the top Australian riders went to ride in New Zealand. George Moore, Athol Mulley and WA Smith were among those who ventured across the Tasman for stints. During his stay in New Zealand, Maynard rode winners for top New Zealand trainer George Green, including the Whangarei Cup on Ole. He also rode for American millionaire owner J de Bloiswack.

After 12 months in New Zealand, Maynard returned to Newcastle and immediately took up where he had left off: winning races — including the important Newcastle sprint, the NJC Newmarket, on Ammanulla. In 1960 he took out his second Newcastle Jockeys' Premiership, a feat he would have had achieved sooner if his services had not been so sought after on the metropolitan tracks and riding overseas. He also attained one of his career ambitions in 1960 when he won the Newcastle Gold Cup for trainer 'Silent' Leo O'Sullivan with his imported English stallion North Row. O'Sullivan had achieved legendary status as the manager of tragic boxing champion Les Darcy. Maynard rode one of his great rides to get North Row home in a titanic struggle with second placegetter Vintage. The horses had staged a two-horse war over the concluding stages of the race. North Row gained the judges' verdict by an eyebrow. The aftermath of this victory saw a jubilant Maynard accept a position as rider for leading trainer Keith Daniels in Singapore and Malaysia.

Shortly before his departure, Maynard was involved in an incident, the aftermath of which gained widespread media coverage. The AJC Derby of 1961 remains as one of the most infamous moments in Australian racing history. Blue Era (Mel Schumacher) and Summer Fair (Tommy Hill) fought out a close two-horse war over the concluding stages up the Randwick straight, with Blue Era crossing the line in front of Summer Fair. But there was more to this tussle than was immediately obvious. In a desperate moment over the concluding stages, Schumacher had grabbed hold of Tommy Hill's leg, held him fast and prevented him from riding his mount out. Hill was naturally incensed, and on returning to weigh in immediately filed a protest. The stewards initially laughed at Hill's claim. Fortunately for him, and unluckily for Schumacher, a new camera had been installed looking down the straight. The film clearly showed Schumacher interfering with Hill over the concluding stages. The protest was upheld. Summer Fair and Tommy Hill were awarded the race and Schumacher was given a life suspension. Eventually, Schumacher's sentence was reduced and he returned to the track.

Only months before, Maynard had faced a similar situation in the last race at Newcastle. Maynard, on board the favourite, was beaten in a tight photo finish. After the race, and wildly angry, he filed a protest against the rider of the winner. Maynard told the stewards that the other rider had held his leg and prevented him from riding out his mount. Steward Bob Dawbarn and his assistants laughed Maynard from the stewards' room. Unlike the Derby, only months later, there was no camera at Newcastle and the result stood — much to Maynard's annoyance. Ironically, the rider who held Maynard's leg that day was none other than Tommy Hill.

Decades later, Merv's wife, Judy, was in the Randwick Members' Enclosure when Tommy Hill sat down next to her. Hill at the time was a very sick man, and it was shortly before his death. He inquired after Judy's and Merv's health. They went on to discuss the merits of different horses on the program, then Tommy said suddenly, 'Judy, sometimes you do things through life for which you are very sorry.' Although Tommy did not refer to the incident directly, Judy knew very well what he was talking about. Years later, in private conversation, Mr Date, the Clerk of the Course, backed up Maynard's claim about that fateful day at Newcastle. On the day, however, he had remained silent because of other officials' derision.

Maynard took up his contract with Keith Daniels and stayed in Asia for over four years. His most important victories were in the Penang Cup on Kerrie Dale and the Sultan's Cup on Kodama. He rode winners for the Sultan of Johor and made many lifelong friends, including Melbourne jockey Ken Smith. One man for whom he rode was wealthy Chinese tin mine owner WS Lim, who took an immediate liking to Maynard and Judy. Lim provided them with the choice of any motor vehicles from his garage. They could drive a Jaguar, a Mercedes and a little red MG sports car. They found it was impossible to look at anything even casually because Lim would immediately be under the impression that they wanted it, and would go ahead and buy it for them.

The downside to Lim was that he was forever at their side – every minute of almost every day. As they didn't want to insult him, this had to be tolerated. One funny highlight of Lim's attraction surfaced when Maynard received a request to ride at Kuala Lumpur. Lim was tied down with business commitments in Singapore, and apologetically begged Maynard and Judy's forgiveness for not being able to accompany them. He provided a plane and saw them off in Singapore. Maynard and his wife rubbed their hands with glee. At last they had given the adoring Lim the slip. That night in their motel room in Kuala Lumpur, the phone rang and Judy answered the call. It was Lim.

'How is the weather in Singapore?' Judy asked him.

'I not in Singapore,' Lim replied.

'Oh, where are you then, Lim?' Judy asked.

He replied enthusiastically, 'I in room next door.'

He had finished his business commitments in Singapore early and arranged a later flight, and said how happy he was to surprise his friends with a late-night dinner. Surprise them he did! Judy Maynard described WS Lim as one of the kindest and most genuine human beings she had ever met. Some years later, his body was discovered in a Hong Kong motel room. Sadly, after the disintegration of his marriage, he had died a lonely man.

Maynard returned to Australia in 1964. His first meeting was in the Upper Hunter at Aberdeen, where he obligingly booted home a treble of winners. However, race riding began to take more of a back seat for Maynard.

With the connections he and Judy had made in the East, they established a thoroughbred bloodstock agency, selling horses to Asia. They sold mainly to Singapore and Malaysia, but also to owners in New Caledonia, Macau, Hong Kong, China, India and South Korea. Maynard began to spend more time tending to their horses and on business trips to Asia, until his involvement with race riding was almost a part-time occupation. But he could not sever his links completely with racing, and the ensuing years continued to see him bring home his share of winners, adding all the time to his already impressive tally of feature race victories on country tracks.

In 1981, Judy Maynard was granted one of the first trainer's permits for a woman and Maynard's riding keenness was rekindled. The pair of them were soon in the winners' list, clocking up wins with Patana and Prince Razzo at Muswellbrook and Newcastle.

The Maynard combination achieved a historical milestone with the grey gelding No Score. The plugging grey won two races at Randwick racecourse. On the first occasion, he was partnered by Jack Thompson when Maynard could not make the weight of 49 kilograms, but in his second victory Maynard rode No Score in the 2000 metre Chester Handicap. This historical moment was the first recorded instance where a trainer/wife and husband/jockey had combined successfully on a metropolitan track, and the Maynards became front-page news.

They received a setback in 1982 when Maynard was heavily thrown and trampled in the saddling enclosure at Newcastle racecourse. He was badly injured, suffering three broken ribs, a broken collarbone and a punctured lung. However, as a professional rider, Maynard was superbly fit. Even having turned 50, he quickly bounced back from his injuries and within three months was back riding winners.

By the Newcastle Cup Carnival of 1983, Merv and Judy Maynard were once more grabbing headlines. The family combined successfully when Maynard rode and won on Mirror Jack in the opening event, the Maiden Handicap. Mirror Jack was trained at Yarra Glen by Kenny Smith, a long-time friend and former jockey. Smith realised early that his young colt showed great potential. He had the horse primed and ready for a first-up plunge. The horse was transferred to Judy Maynard and was driven from Melbourne by Smith himself. Smith met Judy and son John under a street light outside Warwick Farm racecourse at 2 am. The horse was unloaded from Smith's float and loaded on to the Maynards' trailer for the drive to Newcastle.

The cloak and dagger move proved highly successful. Mirror Jack was owned by a group of wealthy Melbourne rails bookmakers, and they proceeded to wreak havoc on the Newcastle bookmakers with this superb and well-kept plunge. They backed Mirror Jack in from 25/1 to 4/1 favourite, and under Merv Maynard's guidance and experienced hands, the horse raced to the front at the jump and scooted away in the straight to win easily by two lengths.

Maynard showed no signs of slowing down in his career, and continued on for the next decade doing what he had always done best: booting home winners. The numbers may not have still been there, but each season the name M Maynard continued to go up first on the semaphore boards at racecourses throughout New South Wales.

Maynard's only regret throughout his illustrious riding career had been the missed opportunity of meeting the Queen in 1952 when, as an 18-year-old, he had won the first Queen's Cup.

Then, one night in early 1992, Judy Maynard answered a late-night call. She was informed that it was the Premier's Department, and it had just received notification from Buckingham Palace that Queen Elizabeth II had made a request for her forthcoming trip to Australia. The Queen had expressed the wish to meet Newcastle jockey Merv Maynard. Forty years after the first running, the Queen was to attend the races at Randwick for the running of the Queen's Cup. She was also to open the new stand at Randwick, and she wanted to meet the man who had ridden the first winner of the event.

MERV MAYNARD MEETS QUEEN ELIZABETH II, 40 YEARS AFTER HIS RANDWICK QUEEN'S CUP. COURTESY MAYNARD FAMILY COLLECTION.

Judy Maynard initially thought that someone was pulling their leg, but a further call from AJC chairman and long-time friend Bob Charley confirmed the royal audience. The Maynards went to Randwick on 22 February 1992 and, before a large Randwick crowd, Maynard shook hands with the monarch. He spent some 40 minutes talking to both the Queen and Prince Phillip, both avid racegoers and horse owners. Maynard even tipped the Royals the winner of the Queen's Cup. Both the Queen and Prince Phillip were impressed that Maynard, at 60, was still riding and getting up the occasional winner.

Maynard handed in his rider's licence on 1 August 1994 at the age of 62. He was regarded as one of Australia's top riders in a period many think of as the golden age of Australian jockeys — an era that included Darby Munro, Billy Cook, Jack Thompson, Neville Sellwood, George Moore, Athol Mulley, Scobie Breasly, Bill Williamson, Jack Purtell and also Englishman Lester Piggott. Maynard rode against them all. In recent years, Merv Maynard has been beset by health problems, but he rates the occasion when he was inducted into the Aboriginal Sports Hall of Fame as one of his proudest achievements.

FRANK REYS WITH THE 1973 MELBOURNE CUP.
COURTESY NEWSPIX.

FRANK REYS

The ups and downs and thrills and spills

TRIUMPHS
Total wins 1329
1973 Melbourne Cup
1970 and 1971 Oakleigh Plate
1962 VRC Oaks
1969 Australasian Cup
Herbert Power Handicap

During a career that was a roller-coaster ride of plummeting down turns and dramatic rises, racecourse hecklers and banter affectionately labelled Frank Reys 'Autumn Leaves' due to his misfortune of always falling.

Reys grew up in a large, happy, loving, close-knit family environment that was sustained by a deep religious faith. He learnt to ride almost before he could walk. His mother gave young Frank and his brothers a pony to share, encouraging them to ride. The boys increased their stable by rounding up wild horses on the Mulgrave River in Far North Queensland. They kept the fastest for races they held on the mud flats and sold the culls to buy feed.

'We used to put two bob in a hat for each starter, and the winner took the lot,' Reys said. He won most of the races, then graduated to become a champion show rider in Cairns.

Reys started his racing career when apprenticed to local trainer Alf Barker in March 1949. He won his first ride on Cruedon at Gordonvale on 30 July 1949. Reys finished his apprenticeship with Gordon Shelly, who introduced the young jockey first to Brisbane racing, then to the Sydney tracks. Reys' stay in Sydney was short, however. He finally moved to Melbourne, where he settled. In Victoria, he built a reputation as a top-class rider, on four occasions riding four winners in a day on Melbourne metropolitan courses. Reys also rode five winners in a day at Moe, a regional course. All five winners were ridden for the same trainer, Alf Sands, who after the fifth win said, 'If I'd known you were going to do THAT I would have had a runner for the last as well!'. He won two Oakleigh Plates in 1970 and 1971 on Dual Choice, the 1962 VRC Oaks on Arctic Star, the 1969 Australasian Cup on Yootha and many other feature races.

But accidents punctuated Reys' career, and on several occasions it seemed as if his riding would be over forever. Reys' first major fall was at Kyneton, late in 1969. It resulted in a broken shoulder and concussion. On his return to racing, he won the MVRC William Reid Stakes on Crewman, but within a week had become part of a four-horse collision at Geelong and fractured his pelvis in two places. Following internal complications, his life was saved during an emergency operation, but nonetheless he was in hospital for three months.

Eighteen months later at Flemington, his mount reared on him, again fracturing his pelvis. This time the road to fitness was longer and more difficult, and Reys considered retirement. However, with his usual fortitude Reys recovered, only to be involved in a car accident that led to a groin operation — and more exercises, aches and pains. At a meeting at Moe, his mount fell heavily, breaking Reys' nose and cheekbone and hardly improving his looks. Reys' face was a mess: 'It hurt when he laughed and it hurt when he didn't, and it was just about as funny as a cruising shark', he said.

Reys spent more time under the surgeon's knife and in hospital. He was about to resume race riding when, on New Year's Day in 1973 while visiting a farm, he tried to free a horse tangled in barbed wire. The animal took fright and trampled him, causing severe shock, deep cuts and other injuries.

The family's bank balance was looking very thin, and it stayed that way for eight long months while they toughed it out and Reys struggled physically and mentally to recuperate. It was a tough time for the family, with wife Noelene begging Reys to retire. Reys remained resolute — he wanted one more crack at the Melbourne Cup — and Noelene and his three children gave him their full support.

His body gradually responded, and fitness returned. This time, his luck had turned. Although receiving minor injuries in an accident when he was driving to Moonee Valley for yet another comeback ride, it was not enough to prevent him from riding and winning on Tauto.

The greatest moment in Frank Reys' career was when he won the Melbourne Cup on Gala Supreme in November 1973. He had participated in nine previous attempts to capture Australia's greatest racing prize, but the closest he had come was a third on Welltown in 1964.

Gala Supreme was owned by Pat Curtain, and prepared by Reys' close and long-time friend Ray Hutchins. Curtain had originally bred a number of horses, including Gala Supreme, at his Huntley Lodge Stud near Sunbury, with the specific purpose of selling them. He had even promised a leading Melbourne bookmaker first offer. The bookie failed to take up the option and refused to buy. Subsequently, the colt was sold through an agent to Mario Giretti, who was happy with his purchase and had the colt gelded. But he was shocked to discover through a routine stable examination that his new acquisition had a poor heart score. Much to his regret, Giretti sought relief from his purchase and Curtain, while he did not accept the veterinarian's findings as final, refunded Giretti's money. He also withdrew the horse from the sale list. 'If he is not 100 per cent, then I don't want to sell him to anyone,' he said. 'I don't believe he has a bad heart, and I'll put him into work and prove it myself.'

Initially, Gala Supreme was trained by Phil Burke at Flemington. But as fate would have it, Burke died only months before the Melbourne Cup. Following Burke's death, Curtain handed the horse to Ray Hutchins to train. Hutchins had always been a close friend, training Gala Crest and many others for Curtain.

Hutchins had immediate results, building on foundations already laid by Burke. Gala Supreme won both at Sandown on a heavy track and at Caulfield when the going was fast. The latter win encouraged Curtain to enter Gala Supreme for the 1973 Caulfield and Melbourne Cups. It seems that he had no real confidence at that stage, but was not without hope. The horse was not wanted by the punting public in the early betting markets for the Cup. He was still at 100/1 with no takers in August, about a month after the weights were issued. Indeed, the final winning double (Swell Time and Gala Supreme) could have been supported at 8000/1.

Late in September, Gala Supreme won the 2000 metre Heatherlie Handicap at Caulfield. He showed that win was no fluke when he ran third in the weight-for-age Turnbull Stakes, at Flemington to Australasia (by Gala Crest) and Dayana. Then followed a win in the Herbert Power Handicap that really delighted the stable. Gala Supreme ran a great race in the Caulfield Cup, but was beaten into second place by the New Zealander Swell Time. On a heavy track, Gala Supreme was run down when appearing to be the winner. 'I thought I had it won. Where do these New Zealanders get them? Our bloke could not be fitter,' Frank Reys commented after the race.

The 1973 increase in Melbourne Cup prizemoney had ensured a good contingent of entrants from New Zealand — indeed, these entrants looked so imposing that they dominated the betting. In many eyes, the Cup was as good as already on a plane out of the country. Glengowan was installed as the favourite after victories in the Captain Cook Stakes at Trentham and a last-stride win at his first Australian start when he beat All Shot in the weight-for-age Caulfield Stakes.

However, the Gala Supreme camp — despite the weight of sustained support for the Kiwis — was growing in confidence. After tasting Caulfield Cup defeat, Hutchins was still quietly confident. He realised that his horse had raced some 10.4 kilometres during the past six weeks. He also realised that Gala Supreme was as fit as he could get him and the biggest danger was seeing the horse go over the top. He recommended that Curtain ignore the experts and leave the horse without another run until the Melbourne Cup, some 17 days distant. 'He doesn't need racing. A hard race could knock him out. I am sure I can keep him fresh without trouble and he might need to be nippy at the start,' the trainer declared.

Pre-race apprehension caught up with Reys. Gala Supreme had drawn the extreme outside at barrier 24. Reys knew he was the oldest jockey in the race, and that this would be his last chance to enter the history books. He kept phoning the trainer to discuss how best to ride Gala Supreme from his position. He and Hutchins discussed options for the race over and over. In Reys' final call, he outlined exactly the tactics he wanted to use. 'He told me he'd be one off the fence in fifth or sixth place going out of the straight. And he went and did it,' the trainer said.

Hutchins was not the only person Reys spoke to that night. Darby McCarthy also received a call to discuss tactical options for his ride. 'Brother you've got the horse, you'll win it,' Darby said.

Reys raced Gala Supreme from his wide alley and took advantage of the field's early pace. After the field had gone about 500 metres, he had the horse over near the rails and in about seventh place.

'I knew then that he was going to be hard to beat,' said Hutchins. 'Frank did his part a treat.'

The race itself was fairly — although not altogether — free of mishaps. Dayana came off worst. He cannoned into the rails when Higgins tried to reef him off the heels of Golden Sam. Dayana severely bruised his ribs and lost any chance he may have had. Audaciter made most of the running, closely attended by Strike Again, and these two still led on the home turn. The first serious challenge came from Daneson, who ran to a clear lead at the distance. But then the stands erupted with a roar from Glengowan's many supporters when the favourite closed on Daneson.

With the winning post in sight, and only 50 metres to go, Reys drove Gala Supreme through a needle-eye opening between Daneson and Glengowan. For a stride or two, the three horses appeared to be in a line, until Glengowan tried to duck in and Harris, who had ridden his horse perfectly up to then, lost control for a stride. In that fraction of time, the Cup was lost and won. Reys gave a sharp cut of the whip. Gala Supreme surged to the line a neck ahead of Glengowan with Daneson a further half-length back.

 *Repercussions over the defeat of Glengowan saw Noel Harris the 18-year old New Zealand apprentice criticised for presenting the race to Gala Supreme. Some claimed that Harris made a serious error of judgement when he did not use the whip as he drew level with Daneson in the straight. He was also blamed for not stopping Gala Supreme from getting through between Daneson and Glengowan. But Harris's owner, Douglas Debreeny, was not throwing mud.*

'Noel Harris rode him perfectly. We've got no complaints,' he said — a good loser indeed. Harris conceded that 'a couple of slight checks' might have cost Glengowan the race.

'I thought I was going to win for sure, when he charged up to the leaders. Then he started to roll, not because he was beaten, but because he has always been inclined to do it. I was waiting for it to happen, and when it did, I pulled him off and Gala Supreme got to the front. He was going on strongly again, but the post came too soon. If I had not pulled him out, he would have interfered with Gala Supreme.'

Reys praised Harris, saying that he rode very fairly. 'He got a split between Daneson and Glengowan, both of whom were going straight. But as he reached the opening, Glengowan hung inwards and Harris pulled out before he interfered with me,' he said.

Asked if he would have protested had Glengowan kept boring in, Reys replied, 'I couldn't have won going on the outside, and I couldn't have won had Glengowan kept coming in.'

In the aftermath, Reys deservedly took centre stage, and for a brief moment held the 100,000-strong Flemington crowd and the entire nation in the palm of his hand with an impassioned speech. His hand trembled as he accepted the microphone and racegoers burst into applause. With tears in his eyes, Reys delivered the longest presentation speech ever heard on an Australian racecourse to a hushed audience. He told of his misfortunes, and the love and loyalty of his friends and family.

'I thank my God, my prayers and my family for their encouragement. This is such a wonderful day. I kept picking myself up off the ground and hoping I would win a Melbourne Cup. It's something every jockey dreams about. I still can't believe it,' he said.

Reys, the quiet-voiced, friendly and rather shy man with the face of a knockabout pixie, had nothing else to prove. In 1976 he won a race at Flemington for Ray Hutchins and immediately put a full stop on his 28-year career, thus

FRANK REYS WITH DAUGHTER SHELLEY (AGED 6) THE MORNING AFTER REYS WON THE 1973 MELBOURNE CUP.
COURTESY SHELLEY REYS.

achieving the milestone of winning both his first and last rides in races. He became involved in a stud venture and then a licensed grocery business, and underwent major surgery for cancer in 1981. His health was very poor and he died in the autumn of 1984, aged 53.

Most, if not all, written racing historical accounts have said that Frank Reys came from a Filipino background. He was described as having overcome an impoverished background, and as having been raised in Cairns as one of 14 children. It is said that his father came to Australia from the Philippines as a corn farmer. The assumption that Reys' parents were Filipino was only partly correct, since many Aboriginal riders were at times forced to disguise their background. Darby McCarthy said of Frank Reys that he was an Aboriginal rider who won a Melbourne Cup. He maintained that there was no doubt — absolutely no doubt at all — about his background. Frank's mob were active members of the local Aboriginal community from up around Cairns and were of mixed Aboriginal/Filipino origins.

Strangely, Reys' victory in the 1973 Melbourne Cup aboard Gala Supreme was tied in a small way to Peter St Albans' victory in 1876. Peter St Albans had won the Cup 97 years earlier on Briseis, a horse from the same family as Gala Supreme. Frank's daughter, Shelley Reys, proudly attended the launch of the first edition of *Aboriginal Stars of the Turf* at Randwick in November 2002.

NORM ROSE

Hopes and dreams

In the late 1950s, a young Aboriginal boy stepped off the train at Broadmeadow station in Newcastle. He had endured a long trip from a little town named Dirranbandi, 960 kilometres west of Brisbane. Norm Rose was just 15 years old, and he was joining the stables of the famed Keith Tinson.

Although not aware of it at the time, Rose was following a tradition: in 1939 Tinson had apprenticed Aboriginal rider Stan Johnson, followed a decade later by Merv Maynard and during the mid-1950s by Gordon Taylor.

Rose had acquired an early love of horses and was a natural rider. He had begun riding station hacks in the dusty outback, where his father worked as a fencer and at any other job required of him. Attending school was out of the question, and lessons were sent each week from Brisbane for Rose to study and return. After his father died, the family had moved to Dirranbandi, where they acquired a house and began a real struggle to survive. Rose worked in a dry cleaners while his mother was employed as a cleaner. Rose also worked overtime and did odd jobs to supplement his income.

Rose began racing for a neighbour and friend of the family, Les Judge, who trained a few racehorses. When on one occasion his regular track work rider failed to appear, he asked Rose whether he would mind riding the horses in their work. Rose was only a kid, but he loved the opportunity of riding and handled himself very well. He had been among horses all his life, and was very comfortable with them. He quickly adapted to what was necessary on the track and Judge kept him on.

His first break came when a friend of his late father — Mr Johnson, the owner of Wyralla Station at Hebel and some of the horses Judge had in training — saw him at work. He asked whether Rose would be interested in going down to Newcastle to Keith Tinson's stable, where Johnson had another horse — a mare called Wanton Lass. The offer seemed too good to pass up, but it was nevertheless a difficult decision to leave his mother and family behind. He was just 15 at the time. Johnson took him to the railway station, put him on the train at Mungindi and he left for Broadmeadow.

It was no easy task leaving Dirranbandi. Rose was a shy young man who had never before been in a city as large as Newcastle and at first it was an intimidating and frightening experience.

But there was an 'atmosphere' about the famous Newcastle establishment. Perhaps it was starting a career where so many good horses — English Standard, Dark Moments, Warrah King, Denali, Paragon — had been prepared. Like others before him, Rose discovered that Tinson was a very hard boss who demanded the best from his staff. Rose lived on the course next to the stables. Tinson would wake him at 3.30 every morning. He would kick the door in and get him out of bed. It was a vastly different environment from the one that apprentices experience today.

'It was pretty hard then. You knew you had to do the right thing and that was it, you had to respect him. He'd go crook if you didn't do the right thing. He'd say "God forgive me". I'll never forget it — it still sticks in my head. He never used to swear, the old boss, it was always, "God forgive me, these boys made me do it".'

Norm would have returned to Dirranbandi with no regrets if his dream of becoming a jockey had not eventuated. But he was willing to put enough effort into being an apprentice, and found that everything fell into place. He was able to ride trackwork almost immediately, and was an instant asset to the stable. Appointed as Wanton Lass's strapper, a bond of affection sprang up between the pair. Johnson would come down from his sheep and cattle property to check on the well-being of both his mare and Norm, generally finding both in good spirits.

Norm missed home, but he loved the racing environment. He was patient while waiting for his first opportunity to ride and did not take long to get among the winners when he did.

Rose had his first success in April 1962 at Newcastle. His first winning ride was on the chestnut Rawson filly Canagle. Later that day, he won on Wanton Lass in a Flying Handicap, defeating Frontlet and Furhoy. Wanton Lass (by Bob Cherry out of Gratia) was a fine sprinter, and showed a touch of class with an excellent fourth in a Doomben Ten Thousand. The Broadmeadow double gave the apprentice a real boost, and things did not seem so bad after all. In any case, Tinson kept him too busy to become homesick.

A steady flow of winners meant that he soon became a favourite with northern punters. Rain, coupled with a bitterly cold wind, didn't prevent them from turning up in force at a Newcastle meeting on 16 May 1964. The renowned Broadmeadow track was virtually a bog as rain continued during the afternoon. But young Rose was in brilliant form, and landed a treble with Willie Win (Maiden), Back to Port (Flying) and Anna's Pal (Intermediate). It was a stable treble too, and the apprentice beamed with delight as he brought Anna's Pal through the downpour and back to the winners' circle.

NORM ROSE. REPRODUCED FROM *DAWN* MAGAZINE, NO. 12, NOVEMBER 1963. COURTESY ABORIGINAL AFFAIRS, OFFICE OF COMMUNITIES, NSW DEPARTMENT OF EDUCATION.

But it didn't matter how many winners he rode, Norm couldn't keep all the punters happy. One day he rode three winners at Broadmeadow, but was beaten on one. Later, when he was walking near the Century movie theatre, going to the Central Cafe for tea because there were no meals down near the stables, a woman chased him with an umbrella.

'You black bastard,' she shouted. 'You pulled that horse up in the last.'

Rose showed a good turn of speed to escape.

In racing, you are only as good as your last winner. Trainers such as Doug Frost would tell the jockey what they had to do and where they had to be, and that when or if they were beaten it didn't matter. They had to ride the race to everything he told them. When the jockey came back in, if the trainer had had a bit on and the horse had won he would be pleased.

'Oh gee, you rode that a good race son,' he'd say.

It might have been different if they had lost, but still they needed to be able to handle the abuse with the praise.

'If you can't handle it son, you better get back on the train because you are going to get plenty more of it. You have to just cop it and just smile. Don't ever put your thumb up at them, just give them a smile, that hurts them more than anything. You are only human and you make mistakes like the rest of them,' Rose's old boss used to say.

But Rose felt that racing eradicated the differences between people. 'If you are a good rider, you are simply a good rider. People abuse the jockey if they lose their money. It made no difference the colour of the jockey's skin — black, white or otherwise. In those days he [the jockey] got on his horse and did his job.'

Being an Aborigine had not made it harder for him to make his way in racing than it was for the average jockey. Jockeys such as George Moore were abused too, even although they were at the top. Rose wasn't worried about being called a 'black bastard'.

Over the years, Rose showed that he was prepared to go to any length or distance to ride a winner. He took his boots and saddle to Grafton, Moree, Mungindi, Hebel, Dirranbandi, St George, Taree, Wyong, Dubbo, Warren, Quirindi and throughout the Hunter Valley. They were great days. He met nice people everywhere he went and enjoyed everything. He found that it did not matter what the place was like: you could still have fun if you rode a winner.

When Norm went to Wallabadah for the first time, Tinson had entered Sadie's Son in an Improvers race. The course was picturesque and tree lined, and the track was celebrating its 118th annual meeting. The long trip to Wallabadah was especially worthwhile, since he won the race.

It was far from easy to be a young jockey in the early days — especially riding in the bush: jockeys had to know what they were doing or they just got lost in the dust. The smart jockeys would know how to beat the young blokes out. They'd talk to them, say something to attract their attention. If they missed the kick they were gone, back in the dust eating the flies in those days.

One time at Tamworth, coming out of the barriers, bush jockey Billy Tracey was leading and Rose was running second. When they came around the turn, the rail was a cutaway because the racing authorities had not moved the fence out. No matter where Tracey went, Rose would get a run. When they came around the turn, the fence ducked in, Rose got up on the inside of him and won the race. When they went back in, Tracey abused him.

'You silly young so and so, don't you ever duck up on the inside of me again like that, or I'll put you over the fence.'

Tracey never had a hope of putting Rose over the fence, because if he had gone in, Rose would have stayed where he was and still had the run.

Jockeys used to get hooked up in the old strand barriers. If they jumped a bit quickly, they nearly got their necks cut off. The iron and steel starting gates followed them. 'Now they have got them all padded up.'

On one of Rose's first visits to ride at Taree, he was surreptitiously helped by Maxie Day, a fellow jockey and a big bloke. Rose was getting his gear ready and the next thing he knew Day had his hand on his back.

'Stay there son,' he whispered as he leaned on Rose's back.

'Correct weight,' the old bloke on the scales said.

When Rose answered a call to ride a horse called Didjeridoo, he thought someone was pulling his leg. He was assured that it was a legitimate engagement and accepted the mount.

'If this wasn't an omen horse, then there never had been one. A blackfella, riding a jet-black horse named Didjeridoo,' Rose reckoned.

And so it proved. Rose and Didjeridoo were a perfect combination. Backed from 14/1 to 3/1, Didjeridoo won the Maiden Handicap, first division by two and a half-lengths from Rose of Mexicano with 5/2 favourite True Grit third a length away. Bookmakers reported one of their worst results on a country course. Rose had Didjeridoo in the leading division all the way, and the black gelding achieved an easy win.

After Rose finished his apprenticeship, he rode in races as a hobby rather than for a full-time job. The money he received from riding put the icing on the cake, providing extra income for his family. He worked first at BHP Newcastle as a crane driver and then with Newcastle Galvanising. In 1974, a man with a young family could not afford to depend on casual income. He had to be certain that there was something coming in each week.

During his riding and working life, Rose got out of bed at 4.30 each morning and after completing his commitments of trackwork riding at Broadmeadow he went straight to work at BHP, where he began at 8 am. He knocked off work at 4 pm and finally, his day over, arrived home had a short period to relax before being in bed by 8 pm. Occasionally he stayed up until 9.30, but he regarded that as a very late night. Rose's riding career was initially supported through Keith Tinson, and he maintained his association with that stable after Tinson's death by riding for his son, Jimmy. Up until Warren Edwards' premature death, he was also supportive of Rose's career, providing both rides and friendship.

Norm Rose reminisced about the many memories and great moments, riders and horses, he'd encountered during his career. He felt that George Moore was the best rider he had come up against. He was just so professional in all he did:

I thought he was a very polished rider, George Moore. I always admired George, you'd go down to Randwick, and he'd always come up and ask what you were riding. He'd look at the colours, he knew everyone in the race. He knew where everyone would be; he could tell what was going on. He never sat still. I always used to take notice of him. I idolised him as a rider. When you got to Sydney and you followed George Moore and them blokes, well you knew where you were going. You knew you weren't going to get into trouble. It was a bit different to following kids in the bush.

Rose rode many horses throughout his long career, but Nook and Royal Rake rate as the best two horses he rode. He won six races straight on Nook. She was a compact filly by Lower Road from Safest. He was with Nook from the time she came into racing, riding her when she came into the stable after being broken in. Both Jimmy Tinson and Rose always thought she showed a lot of promise. She demonstrated above-average ability the first time they put her down, and she just continued on with it. Nook won a series of races in 1973 at Newcastle, Gosford, Canterbury and Rosehill. She was voted Newcastle's 'Horse of the Year' for the 1973–74 season. She also won a series of open sprints, beating the track record at Rosehill. Only Zephyr Bay could match her speed. By February 1975, she had notched up 13 wins.

'You only dream about one like her. She appeared to be just coasting at Rosehill. I got the shock of my life to learn the record for the 1200 metres had been smashed,' Rose reflected.

One of the highlights of Rose's career was when he rode Nook in the Newmarket Handicap at Flemington. He thought he had a good chance 50 metres out. Then he looked across the track and there was a wall of horses going to the line. In this thundering finish, Nook finished unplaced.

Royal Rake may well have proven to be the best of all Rose's mounts, but he was tragically killed after a fall in the Country Cup at Randwick. Rose felt that Royal Rake could have been anything, and believed he could have won the 1963 Metropolitan. Royal Rake, Nadar Shah and Tarberry fell in the Country Cup, with Royal Rake having to be destroyed.

Fortunately, Rose's career did not see many serious falls; his worst was in fact the one at Randwick on Royal Rake. There were 20 runners in the race, and he was on the fence when four of them came down. He went over the top of WA Smith because there was nowhere else to go. He wore a new fibreglass helmet that had just come in, and it split clean from front to back. If he had had the old helmet on, which just used to slip over the jockey's head with no chin guard, he would have been killed. As it was, Rose just had a sore neck for a few weeks.

When Rose was an apprentice, he rode once a fortnight since his old boss only let him ride at Newcastle. Now apprentices race every day of the week and can earn a reasonable amount of money if they are keen enough and want to ride. Although Rose would still like to be riding, time does not stand still. 'When you get old you have to know when it is time to stop,' he said.

RICHARD LAWRENCE 'DARBY' McCARTHY

Jockeys, trainers, apprentices, strappers and racetrack banter

TRIUMPHS
Australian Jockey Club Derby
Australian Jockey Club Epsom Handicap
Australian Jockey Club Tancred Stakes
Brisbane Cup
Doomben Ten Thousand
Three Stradbroke Handicaps
Newcastle Cup
Many other group and listed races

Darby McCarthy was an Aboriginal jockey who was proud of his origins. He was also blessed with a quick and ready wit.

'No, I'm black, you're coloured. I was born black, stay black and die black. You're born pink, go white, get brown in the sun and finally end up grey.'

The son of a Cunnamulla Aboriginal stockman, Darby McCarthy was the eighth child in a family of 12: six boys and six girls. He gained an early education on horseback riding brumbies on a Cunnamulla station. At the age of 9, to help support his large family, he went to work at Yakara Station, about 50 kilometres south-west of Thargomindah in Queensland.

Yakara was owned by Mr Charlie Easton, a keen racing man. McCarthy's job was to round up horses for the stockmen before the start of each working day. With his mother, five brothers and six sisters, he lived in a tent on the property.

McCarthy displayed a natural talent on horseback, with his balance and skill very evident to those who saw him in the saddle. He could ride wild calves and brumbies as well as any of the senior riders. When he was 12, Darby was taken to a small picnic race meeting at Thargomindah by his father and Charlie Easton.

DARBY McCARTHY LOOKING EASY IN THE SADDLE. COURTESY NEWSPIX.

'I was given the ride on Rusty in a 5 furlong (1000 metre) sprint. He jumped straight as a gun barrel at the start and led all the way.'

His winning ride impressed an enthusiastic Easton, who nicknamed him 'Darby' after the famed jockey Darby Munro.

Many years later, Darby McCarthy reflected upon some of those early years in the saddle to racing journalist Tony Arrold, including a humorous incident at a meeting in Cunnamulla:

> The owner had arrived at the dusty track in a bit of a flap, having forgotten to pack his racing silks of white jacket with black spots, white cap.
>
> One look at young McCarthy and the owner solved the problem. He found a white shirt and began to cut out circles from the cotton material. Then he threw the shirt over the narrow shoulders of the tiny jockey standing before him.
>
> White jacket, black spots. The dark brown eyes of 'Darby' McCarthy lit up and his lips parted in the widest of grins.

95

Wearing his custom-made silks, McCarthy duly rode the horse a treat as they streeted the opposition and helped connections clean up the bookies.

Young McCarthy was not without advisers. His eldest brother, Ted, had built up a fine reputation as a good jockey, especially in the Toowoomba area, until weight problems curtailed his career. Ted was anointed with the name 'Scobie'.

> Highlight of the first day of the centenary meeting was the success of a 15-year-old aboriginal jockey, E. 'Scobie' McCarthy …
>
> McCarthy won a race on the former Brisbane galloper, Rewi Pete, and finished a close second on Bussarang in the principal event — the Charleville Flying …
>
> The lad shows splendid promise in the saddle and old timers here say that he is easily the best aboriginal jockey to have ridden in the west in many years.
>
> — *The Charleville Times, 7 November 1947*

Ted 'Scobie' McCarthy was a top rider, and it may have been a colour bar that limited his riding opportunities. Some said that the elder McCarthy was prevented from riding any further east than Dalby in Queensland.

Fortunately for Darby McCarthy, his own career started off in a period of tumultuous and dramatic change. The 1960s brought television to many homes. People witnessed the enormously divisive war in Vietnam, a highly visible and active American civil rights movement and the Cold War. These events inspired Aboriginal people to organise and speak out about the injustices being brought against them daily.

In the 1960s, Aboriginal activist Charles Perkins organised Australia's equivalent of the American civil rights 'Freedom Rides'. A highly visible and active Aboriginal political voice began to be heard as Aborigines marched and voiced their opinions. The 1967 referendum contributed to belated acknowledgement of Aborigines as citizens in their own country. Aboriginal sportsmen and women have made visible and positive contributions in the ongoing journey of recognition.

Darby McCarthy may have been fortunate to have followed his brother and many others into an era of greater awareness and opportunity, but that does not detract from the unquestioned talent that he possessed. McCarthy was gifted, but prone to bouts of erratic and unpredictable behaviour and falling foul of officialdom. In 1958, while in Brisbane visiting his sick father, young Darby attended a race meeting at Albion Park. He was standing watching the horses parade in the saddling enclosure when he came under the gaze of well-known trainer Ted Hennessy. Ted was not slow in coming forward and, having noticed young Darby's interest, immediately asked him whether he needed a job. The gleam in Darby's eyes was all the confirmation Hennessy needed, and McCarthy became apprenticed in October 1958. At only his third professional ride, he was victorious at Kilcoy.

Darby McCarthy had begun his climb to the top of racing. He rode his first city winner at Doomben on the 50/1 chance Rio Sand. In 1960, Darby was dux of the Queensland Turf Club's Apprentice School, and he was presented with a saddle by the Governor of Queensland, His Excellency Sir Abel Smith.

In contrast to many early Aboriginal jockeys, McCarthy was proud to be recognised as Aboriginal. In response to a complaint from a newspaper reader about reporters continually referring to McCarthy as Aboriginal, he replied:

> I think the man is sincere and trying to be fair but he misses the whole point. If any newspaperman wants to do me a favour he can call me an Aborigine as often as he mentions my name — because that is what I am, and if I am going to be a success it is important that I be known as an Aboriginal success.

In his first three years in the saddle, Darby chalked up over a hundred winners in Queensland, New South Wales and Victoria. Feature races were not long in coming to the talented rider. He won the 1960 Brisbane Summer Cup on Midswain and the 1960 Brisbane Tattersalls Cup on Melbourne galloper Dow Street.

In 1961, McCarthy journeyed to Melbourne for the Spring Carnival, partnering Dow Street in the Melbourne Cup; he escaped unscathed when the horse fell.

By this time, Darby was spending a lot of time riding at important meetings in New South Wales. He was victorious on the Mal Barnes-trained Alspick in the 6 furlong (1200 metre) Ramornie Handicap at Grafton.

In 1962, while still an apprentice, McCarthy moved south again, partnering Tamure to win the Newcastle Gold Cup for Warwick Farm trainer Norman Turnbull. McCarthy's association with Alspick now hit a purple patch. In December 1962, they combined to win the AJC Summer Cup by eight lengths. McCarthy rode a great race hugging the fence, and was never worse than fifth. Alspick was steered through needle-eye openings to race away with the event. They backed up on New Year's Day 1963 to win the Tattersalls Club Cup.

McCarthy next formed a strong association with the Bobby Sinclair-trained Mullala. On his first six rides on the horse, he recorded five wins, including a brilliant victory in the $20,000 Stradbroke Handicap. With his apprenticeship coming to a close and his services so sought after in the south, McCarthy transferred to Norman Turnbull's Warwick Farm stables to chase greater opportunities to establish himself with major trainers and owners.

McCarthy returned home to Queensland in 1964, now a fully fledged jockey, and repeated his previous year's victory by guiding Cele's Image to victory in the Stradbroke. In 1965, he rode Patient Polly to victory in the Grafton Cup and won the Canterbury Cup on Rakia. In 1966, he took out the rich Brisbane double when he partnered Castanea to victory in yet another Stradbroke and scored a great victory on Apa in the Brisbane Cup. McCarthy went into celebration mode and bought himself a diamond tiepin and cufflink set worth $5000.

McCarthy decided to see the world, with Europe his first port of call. The press back in Australia had a field day as they kept the public at home informed about the whereabouts of 'Dapper' Darby McCarthy. He went to the races at Royal Ascot in a Rolls Royce, complete with top hat and tails. George Moore won the Derby on Royal Palace that year. Darby didn't have a ride on the day, and it was with Moore's encouragement that he donned a Moss Brothers tuxedo and set off to Ascot. Moore had said, 'You're an Indigenous Aboriginal Australian. Let's do you up and go to the Derby.'

McCarthy was attending parties with Mia Farrow and Frank Sinatra. He got drunk with Lee Marvin and Rock Hudson. When McCarthy decided to set up base in France, he was besieged by contract offers. He finally accepted an offer from top French trainer Maurice Zilber, who trained for international art entrepreneur Daniel Wildenstein. The contract was lucrative — including a retainer, bonuses for prizemoney, car and lavish home complete with a French maid in Chantilly. The boy from the bush had arrived, as he wore $400 pale-blue suits to the races. McCarthy rode for the Rothschilds and Prince Aly Khan, and in races in France, Germany, England and Ireland. It was a world far removed from a tent on Yakara Station:

> At Cunnamulla, we lived between the cemetery and the sewerage outlet, mate. Blacks weren't allowed up in the town mind you. What's even more important, I could not even vote in my own country, brother.

Homesickness prompted McCarthy to return to Australia in 1968, and he took out the 1968 Doomben Ten Thousand on Gay Gauntlet. In one golden afternoon at Randwick's 1969 AJC Carnival, Darby McCarthy annexed the two premier events, taking out the AJC Derby on Divide and Rule and in the very next race riding Broker's Tip to an exhilarating victory in the AJC Epsom

Handicap. McCarthy rode a treat on Divide and Rule, being placed so beautifully throughout that he enjoyed a travel-free passage throughout the race:

> The gates opened and from 18 draw, whack I'm one off the fence first time past the winning post and guess what horse pulls its nose up on the inside and alongside my horse's girth. 'Darb, Darb'. 'Yeah George [Moore], he hangs in George.' Because in the Guineas, the horse had hung in I'd told Dick Roden and Neville Begg. I'd had white paint on my boots. 'Hangs in George'. So I went down the hill and round the corner, 'Darb, Darb, yeah I know you're there George', and up to the mile post, mile turn and George dropped back a little bit and I'd moved to around third. So I'm sitting there and had a little lunch and a smoke and we go past the railway side and I just went click, click and we won the race by about four lengths.

The 25-year-old McCarthy and Divide and Rule coasted to the line some five lengths clear of the field.

The victory on Broker's Tip in the Epsom was even more impressive. Trapped in a tight pocket for more than two-and-a-half furlongs (500 metres), McCarthy forced a passage hooking out from behind four runners to charge down the outside and snatch victory from Roy Higgins and Alrello. In the wake of his victories racing journalist Tom Brassel reported that McCarthy 'the glamour jockey' of the AJC Spring Carnival would donate his next winning jockey percentage to the Aboriginal Education Advancement Society. McCarthy, extremely proud of his heritage, appealed to punters who backed his wins in the Derby and Epsom to also make a small contribution to assist Aboriginal educational initiatives. McCarthy also arranged to meet with two of the Aboriginal students.

Darby McCarthy had reached the heights of his profession. However, the fairytale that reached its zenith that afternoon at Randwick began to form into something more akin to a nightmare as McCarthy's career hit a spiral roller-coaster descent:

> I've been right up on top and I've been way down there at the bottom.
> And, baby, believe me, it's a lot better being up.

McCarthy had drank champagne with aristocracy and at one time owned 20 tailor-made suits, but with the nosedive in his career, McCarthy's flash lifestyle was beginning to have an adverse affect. The drop accelerated further in the mid-1970s, when Victorian stewards disqualified him for seven years for allegedly conspiring to fix a race at a lowly mid-week meeting at Hamilton in Western Victoria. The stewards' report stated that McCarthy's mount had interfered with the beaten favourite. On 18 June, the Hamilton racing club charged McCarthy and trainer

Bob Smeardon with a number of offences. Stewards had spent over six hours deliberating over accusations and evidence, and it was reported that an unnamed individual who failed to appear before the inquiry would also be charged.

The investigation had been set in progress by George Rantall, the trainer of the beaten favourite. He alleged that he had been approached to 'slow' the favourite. The inquiry went into its eleventh hearing before the stewards announced that jockey McCarthy had been disqualified for seven years, Bob Smeardon relinquished his trainer's licence and the unnamed person was warned off racecourses for life.

McCarthy strongly denied any wrongdoing on his part, and pleaded his innocence in any plot, but it all fell on deaf ears. This is the worst situation a jockey can encounter, and McCarthy fought to clear his name. He lodged an appeal with the South Western District Racing Association and, largely with the help of a group of top lawyers — including later Victorian Premier John Cain and Victorian State Ombudsman Sir John Dillon — his sentence was reduced to two years. McCarthy never gave up the fight. Following further appeals, the disqualification was eventually dropped and all references were removed from McCarthy's record. When filling in the form for his return to race riding, he asked whether he should put in the disqualification when he went to get another licence.

'No. It has been removed. There was no disqualification,' was the reply.

McCarthy could not believe it.

'Well if I haven't been disqualified, where is my house, my money and why haven't I been able to make a living from racing for 10 months?'

Insurmountable damage had been done. The calls for rides were no longer there, and backslappers — only too pleased to associate with a winner — were no longer anywhere to be found. The episode had ruined McCarthy's marriage and he had begun to drink. To make matters worse, since McCarthy had continued to spend in the fashion to which he had been accustomed, the money was also soon all gone. His life had been so simple before. He would ride a few winners, fill his pockets with money and go out and buy cars and houses. When it ran out, he would do it all over again.

But now times were different. The damage to his reputation was significant and the horses simply were not there any more. Without the good mounts, there was no avenue to rise back up and replenish the coffers. McCarthy started selling off his property to get money. He even sold his much-valued tie pin and cufflinks, which fetched only $1250. McCarthy found himself at odds with the police.

'I'd have a drink and I'd be a zombie, talking duck talk. People would see me and reckon I was on the grog heavy.'

He was also faced with every jockey's dread: increasing weight troubles. Weight had always been a really big problem for him. A friend put him on prescription drugs, which he swallowed like smarties to keep his weight down. But jockeys were never warned of the dangers of mixing those kinds of drugs with drink. He discovered the body of his young brother dead after an overdose of prescription drugs.

An attempted comeback with Victorian master trainer of 2-year-olds, Cliff Fahler, came to a crashing end. McCarthy — still walking the tightrope of mixing weight-reducing drugs and alcohol — had put his arm through a plate-glass window and nearly severed it. The arm was saved, but with restricted movement in the left wrist. Under enormous strain, McCarthy buckled under the weight of his decline and was admitted to a psychiatric ward for evaluation. On his discharge, he booked himself into a drug and alcohol rehabilitation centre.

'I walked on the wild side, there's no doubt about that,' he said.

McCarthy dried out and began the slow climb back out of his own personal hell. He overcame obstacles related to his arm to once more gain a rider's licence, and in 1978 made another comeback — this time in New Caledonia. When he returned to Sydney, he renewed his long-time association with Mal Barnes. He seemed to be back on track, and struck up a good partnership with a horse named Hyperno, with which he combined to take out the 1978 STC Tancred Stakes. Sadly, it was only a short-lived return. He wasted hard and got his weight down to 54.5 kilograms, but still wasn't getting any rides.

'It didn't seem worth it. I couldn't do it any more.'

McCarthy remarried, then he packed up and headed back to Queensland to begin a new life as a trainer. With the backing of old friend Lloyd Foyster, he set up a training centre out of Toowoomba's Clifford Park course. On 18 February 1984, he won his first race as a trainer when the 15/1 shot Ptah was first past the post. McCarthy began with 14 boxes and, with further additions from the Foyster string, things looked rosy.

But he was not content. Through the then Commonwealth Department of Aboriginal Affairs, he planned to take in young Aboriginal kids and teach them the art of horsemanship. After his expert tuition, these young people would be well placed to go out into the razor-edge world of racing, equipped both mentally and physically to face the perils of big-time racing. McCarthy also wanted to see young Aboriginal kids gain similar opportunities to those he had been given. It was something he had always wanted to do: pass on the knowledge he had built up for himself.

'I kept thinking how many other young black kids would have made something of their lives if they had been able to do this sort of thing.'

McCarthy received the necessary departmental backing and support for his project. He was enthusiastic: under the scheme, he would have boys in his care for some 13 weeks. During that time, they would receive tuition on every aspect of life in and around a racing stable, including learning to ride, mucking out stables, grooming, shoeing, feeding and horse care. McCarthy was firm with the boys, saying that they also needed to learn to do as they were told. He took them to the track each morning, attended race meetings with them and showed them videos. They discussed what they were shown.

Two apprentices — Courtney Appo and McCarthy's nephew, David McCarthy came through the instruction and were immediately able to secure apprenticeships. Sadly, after some three years of operation, the apprentice school disbanded. McCarthy was disillusioned with the lack of drive and commitment of many of the boys. He also found the life of a trainer — particularly the challenges of having to deal with owners — a far more cut-throat world than that of a top jockey.

In 1987, he unsuccessfully stood as the Australian Democrats candidate for the seat of Maranoa in Queensland in the general election.

Today, McCarthy is forthright in his opinions about the problems facing his people and country:

> I believe it was then, and is today, an attitude problem. It's very hard to capture a country and not understand the culture of a country. You need that time to digest and understand it fully and accept it, deal with it. This country has not dealt with it properly or fairly in any way. For a couple of hundred years, there were just no blacks in this country. We have lived a lie for just over 200 years.
>
> Now they still haven't dealt with our law, they still haven't dealt with our education. And they have got to think about reconciliation. They're running around saying 'We'll reconcile this we'll reconcile that', like ducky! You just can't grab a culture and law, that is one of the oldest in the world bar none and fix it all up in 20 or 30 years. You can't do that.
>
> Unfortunately a lot of government and a lot of our people believe you can. What are we reconciling? It's supposed to have been a war? There's been no war. There's just been murder and a mass genocide of this country and our people and finally after a couple of hundred years, 'Yeah alright, there were people here, no more Terra Nullius anymore'.

At the age of 45, Darby McCarthy made one more attempt at a comeback as a jockey. On 28 July 1990, he was re-licensed by the Queensland Turf Club committee. When given the news, McCarthy was elated and the very next day saw him return to race riding at Brisbane's Doomben Racecourse. His mount finished unplaced but McCarthy was nevertheless ecstatic.

'It's hard turning your life around after 10 years but the old touch is still there and I want to ride.'

Despite McCarthy's enthusiasm and commitment to the task, the stark realities soon came to the fore. Although the heart was willing, the body was no longer up to the task. McCarthy once more — and for the last time — pulled up the shingles on what was a remarkable career. Looking back over his years in the saddle and reflecting on his ups and downs, McCarthy could still declare about racing:

> Yeah, yeah it didn't matter if you were a Bunker Hunt, a Wildenstein or a Royal Queen. If your horse was good enough it didn't matter. The caviar was seated with the fish and chips.
>
> I suppose there wouldn't be a handful of horsemen jockeys in my opinion. You've got jockeys and you've got horsemen jockeys. They've got to be a horseman to understand the animal that they are working with. Today it's a big machine. The big magic dollar. The jockeys [have] got managers and blokes working with computers, doing times, distances and track conditions. Back in the 1960s when Mulley and I were talking about jockeys' managers, we were considered as being a bit dumb in even mentioning the concept.

In 2009, a partnership formed between Racing NSW and TAFE witnessed the launch of the Darby McCarthy Aboriginal Employment and Training Program. The strategy, fittingly named after one of racing's all-time great jockeys, Darby McCarthy, was designed to provide Indigenous people with pre-vocational training, support and assistance to obtain and maintain a job — including traineeships and apprenticeships in the racing industry. On completion of the training, Racing NSW agreed to facilitate job placements for all successful participants.

Redfern-based Yarn'n Aboriginal Employment Services also assisted, working with the Racing NSW/TAFE partnership to ensure that training of all recruits was conducted using best practice for Aboriginal and Torres Strait Islander people. The first Darby McCarthy Program, conducted in May 2009, was a resounding success, with an astounding 88 per cent of the first group of graduates still in employment 12 months later.

To be eligible for the training, applicants must be Aborigines or Torres Strait Islanders and have a genuine love of horses. Previous riding skills are not essential, nor are there any educational requirements. It is hoped that the program will ensure that some Aboriginal riding talent will follow in the footsteps of the legendary McCarthy. Apprentice winning jockey Darcy Matthews is walking proof of how the program has changed lives. The 17-year-old entered a Racing NSW pre-vocational training program with no previous horse experience. Twelve months on, Matthews notched a winning double at his very first race meeting as an apprentice jockey under trainer Jason Coyle.

For his part, Darby looked back over many decades at the track and concluded, 'Well, I've had a good walk. The horses mate, all the lovely horses and lovely rides, it was all due to them.'

LEIGH-ANNE GOODWIN

> Racing is dangerous for jockeys and horses alike. Death always lurks in its background. Yet one is never prepared for its arrival.

TRIUMPHS
The first Aboriginal female jockey to win a metropolitan race

She came from a racing background. Norm Rose was her uncle and Darby McCarthy was a long-time family friend. Her parents are both trainers.

Leigh-Anne Goodwin was Australia's first female Aboriginal jockey to ride a winner at a metropolitan track. She was a beautiful young girl who had a deep love of both horses and racing, and was also extremely proud of her Aboriginal heritage. On 5 December 1998, Leigh-Anne Goodwin had an horrific fall at Roma in Queensland. She sustained extensive head and internal injuries and died two days later in a Brisbane hospital.

Goodwin had to overcome parental disapproval to become a jockey. Racing is a physically demanding career, and in most instances it does not give just rewards for the enormous effort put in. Industry bias against female riders was another hurdle to be overcome. Goodwin juggled these negatives with her role as a single mother of her young son to make her mark as a rider of great talent, potential and commitment.

Goodwin had her heart and soul set on a career as a jockey from the age of 4, and she was apprenticed to her father — trainer Mark Goodwin — at 19. Early disillusionment saw Goodwin move away from racing, and she spent four years completing an apprenticeship as a hairdresser. During this time, she put on weight and took an overseas holiday. Racing was the thing furthest from her

LEIGH-ANNE GOODWIN IN HER SILKS.
COURTESY OF NEWSPIX.

mind. Mark Goodwin had thought he was winning the battle when Leigh-Anne had entered the hairdressing course after school.

On her return to Queensland, Goodwin visited Darby McCarthy, a long-time friend of the family. McCarthy passed on some wisdom from his years at the track. He told her to go the way her mind wanted, and to be happy within herself. The rest, he said, would come naturally. Goodwin had the racing bug reignited and she set about returning to the track. She established herself at Roma in south-western Queensland. She coped with a failed marriage and the birth of her son, and never lost sight of her goals and love of the racetrack.

When she returned to riding, Mark emphasised that she needed a high level of competitive commitment.

'Well if you're going to do it you've got to ride like a man. You're in a man's game and you've got to be able to ride like one,' he said. 'I really think to this day that she held her own.'

The involvement of Goodwin's parents in racing, and her general horse background, had a major impact on her. When Leigh-Anne's father, a former buck-jump rider, suffered a broken back and neck when a horse he was riding crashed down a ditch at a country property, the Goodwins needed an income. Leigh-Anne's mother, Barbara, took out a trainer's licence and in 1989 created history when she became the first female Aboriginal trainer to lead in a metropolitan winner in Brisbane. She has saddled up five horses at a country meeting for five winners. When Mark recovered, both Goodwins held trainers' licences.

The serious and high-risk nature of being a jockey was hammered home to Goodwin in 1995 when her cousin Bill, also a jockey, was left a quadriplegic after a race fall at Dalby.

But Goodwin proved that she was small, petite *and* tough. In May 1997, she rode in the first two races at Augathella, and then was rushed to hospital after suffering an asthma attack. She displayed great tenacity by returning to the track late in the day to honour a prior commitment to ride for a trainer because no other riders were available to take the mount.

By late 1998, Leigh-Anne Goodwin had clocked up 127 career winners. In September 1998, she achieved her proudest moment on the racecourse when she was successful on Getelion at Brisbane's Eagle Farm Racecourse. Her parents owned and trained Getelion, and both were on hand to share in the victory celebration. Getelion was a long-priced outsider in the field, but Goodwin punched him home for a convincing victory.

'That was my ambition: to win a race in the city with the whole family involved,' she said.

After the victory, Goodwin acknowledged that she owed it all to her father and the inspiration of Darby McCarthy. Getelion's form had improved on the bush and picnic racing circuit. It may have been an unusual preparation for Getelion, but the 8-year-old obviously appreciated plenty of racing and travelling.

'Dad started him on the Friday at the picnics over 1200 metres, where he ran third before backing up the next day to win a 1600 metres race,' Goodwin said. 'It's an unorthodox preparation for any city race, but it worked!'

The win on Getelion would sadly remain a monument to Leigh-Anne Goodwin's aspiring career. On 5 December 1998, she suffered severe head and internal injuries in a race fall at Roma. Bachelor King, the horse she was riding, fractured a leg when racing as joint leader about 200 metres after the start of the 1200 metre race. Goodwin was thrown head first into the track, and was struck by following horses.

Two days later, her distraught parents were left with no other alternative than to inform the medical professionals to turn off the life-support machine. Mark Goodwin acknowledged that it was one of his daughter's wishes that if she were involved in a fall where she was severely injured, she did not want to be left a vegetable. She had discussed it with them and made them promise they wouldn't go soft if the hard decision had to be made. She didn't want to just exist.

'Leigh-Anne had seen a few other jockeys like Billy Barnes and Merv Marion go on for ages even though they had serious brain injuries. She didn't have a premonition about having an accident like this. She was just being realistic,' said Leigh-Anne's sister, Jemimah.

Mark and Barbara Goodwin, and Jemimah, bravely faced the media after their heart-wrenching decision, and they recalled the daughter who just wouldn't take no for an answer when it came to choosing a career.

'Leigh-Anne was an inspiration to the Aboriginal children who knew her, and upon her death we received many wonderful letters from distinguished Aboriginal people,' Jemimah said. 'Unfortunately, it took her death to attract the kind of attention she deserved — as a sporting person extremely proud of the fact that she was Aboriginal.'

Leigh-Anne inherited her capacity to overcome the pockets of racial and gender discrimination in the horse-racing industry from her very determined mother.

'Mum faced a lot of discrimination, and so did Leigh-Anne — there were certainly no advantages given to either of them,' Jemimah said. 'They both had to fight harder and constantly prove themselves, firstly because they were women, and secondly because they were Aboriginal women in a white male-dominated industry.'

Over 1500 people attended Leigh-Anne Goodwin's funeral in Toowoomba. Her memory and legacy have stayed with us.

PART III
AHEAD OF THE FIELD: MORE INDIGENOUS AUSTRALIAN JOCKEYS

CHARLIE FLANNIGAN

In 1881, an Aboriginal horseman named Charlie Flannigan was a stockman in a cattle drive of 20,000 head from Richmond Downs in Queensland to the Northern Territory. The route of the drive followed an Aboriginal road, which later became the main stock route to the Northern Territory between Burketown and Borroloola. It gained the foreboding name of the Hell's Gate Track. Charlie Flannigan was a capable jockey who won the 1887 Palmerston Cup on Cygnet. As a jockey, he rode in both official and unofficial race meetings at Playford, Pine Creek, Yam Creek, Brocks Creek, Borroloola, Wyndham and Halls Creek. He rode right across the Northern Territory, Western Australia and Queensland.

Flannigan spent most of his young life in the company of wild horsemen, cattle and horses on the northern frontier of the colony. He was born in 1865 at Richmond Downs near the township of Richmond in north Queensland. He worked at the Ord River Station, Wave Hill Station, Victoria River Downs and many more cattle stations that were dotted across the Top End, doing odd jobs as a general roustabout. He was recognised for his skills as a horseman, strapper, stablehand and jockey.

On 20 September 1892, Flannigan was charged with the murder of Samuel Croker (aka Greenhide Sam) over a card game. He was incarcerated in Fannie Bay Gaol in Darwin until he was hanged on 15 July 1893. While awaiting trial, he drew and sketched from memory his experiences as a drover. These visual works provide a valuable window on life as a stockman from the late 1800s. Flannigan was the first man to be hanged at Fannie Bay Gaol. His hanging created a public furore about capital punishment.

— *Dale Kerwin*

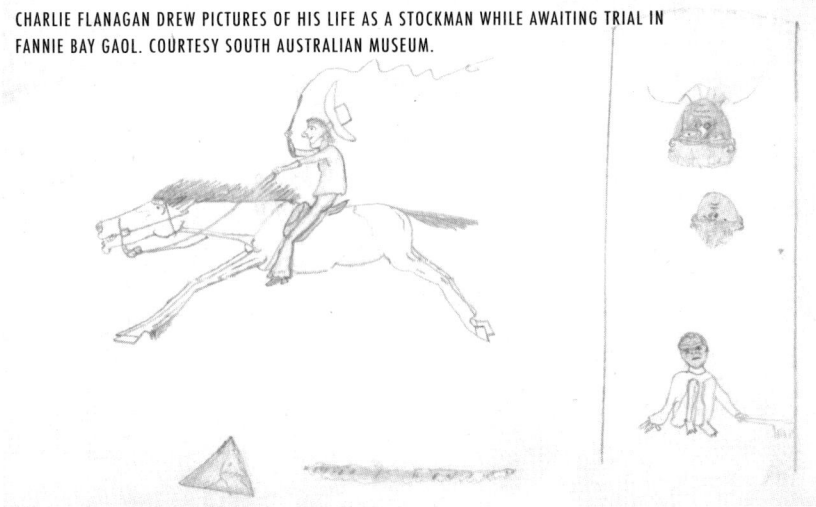

CHARLIE FLANAGAN DREW PICTURES OF HIS LIFE AS A STOCKMAN WHILE AWAITING TRIAL IN FANNIE BAY GAOL. COURTESY SOUTH AUSTRALIAN MUSEUM.

PERCY KENNEDY

I acknowledge the recent family history work undertaken by Wiradjuri woman Denise Hayes to uncover another great forgotten Aboriginal jockey, Percy Kennedy. Percy was Denise Hayes' grandmother's brother, and was born in 1874 at Warangesda mission at Darlington Point in southern New South Wales.

While many members of the family stayed at Warangesda, Percy set off to Melbourne, chasing his dream to become a jockey. He established himself as a top-class steeplechase jockey in the 1890s, attached to the stables of Mr JE Brewer. Bobby Lewis, one of the all-time greats of Australian racing — including winning the Melbourne Cup four times — had high regard for Percy as a horseman. In his memoirs, Lewis wrote that Percy was 'a racing identity and a fine horseman', adding, 'I suppose everyone who has had much to do with racing in Victoria knows the dark-skinned Percy.'

Percy married a white woman, and by the twenty-first century he would have been all but been forgotten by the family if not for Denise Hayes' diligent research, which placed him not just back into his family but also restored him to his rightful place in Australian racing history.

He rode in Melbourne, Perth and Brisbane, and a newspaper record stands as a testament to his horsemanship and courage on the track:

> In connection with the fight between Selim and Forward at Caulfield last week (says *The Sportsman*) a specially plucky bit of work has escaped notice. While the horses were at their maddest Percy Kennedy, the coloured lad who rode Selim when he won his first welter race, rode up to the fighters and at great risk seized Forward by the nostrils. The horse reared up suddenly, dragged Kennedy out of the saddle, and tried to trample on him. But the lad held on in the gamest possible manner, and succeeded in parting the fighters. The opinion of an eyewitness is that, but for Kennedy's gameness, Selim and Forward would have torn one another to pieces.
> — *Brisbane Courier*, 22 December 1894

Percy had only one child — a son who was born in 1897, also named Percy. He volunteered for the first AIF on 6 July 1915 and died of tuberculosis in England on 16 September 1916. Prior to this, he had served in Egypt and France.

Percy Jnr was under age — only 18 — when he volunteered and his father's consent is recorded with his enlistment papers. His mother had died before the war. However, a comparison of this letter of consent with later correspondence between Percy Snr and AIF base records suggests that the consent letter could in fact have been written by the younger Percy.

The letters in the service record of his son are the last evidence of the existence of Percy Kennedy. Denise Hayes continues to chase material on this remarkable jockey.

MASSA READ

Massa Read was a top-class rider from the Tamworth area in northern New South Wales during the early decades of the twentieth century. He was probably born at Narrabri, and was apprenticed to George Cushion. When he retired from race riding, he went back to Narrabri.

Read was a good horseman, always a very light weight in the saddle and the leading rider of his day.

His skin was jet black in colour, and he always rode on an all-white saddle. But he would not go to Sydney to race because of fear of negative crowd reaction to his obvious colour. Nonetheless, Massa Read locked horns with top jockeys such as Jim Pike and Rae Johnstone when they went to the bush.

JIMMY DRIES

Jimmy Dries' first race ride was in the Flying Handicap at Tamworth, when he rode Potter's Field to victory. The year was 1918 and he was 13 years old. Dries was apprenticed to George Cushion in a big stable located in Tamworth, and he learnt from champion rider Massa Read.

Dries was sensitive to his racial background. His wife's family had disowned her because she had married an Aboriginal man. Dries used to disguise his background, saying that he was an Islander.

Dries rode for a little over ten years over an area from Canberra to Bourke, and nearly every place in between. In those days, there were no horse trailers or big truck floats. A trainer would tie his horses to the back of the sulky and go off to a meeting — wherever he had his horses nominated. It sometimes meant a day or a week of travelling.

On one occasion, Dries rode three horses at Tamworth for a trainer named Jack Cavanagh. As soon as the meeting was finished, Cavanagh tied the horses to the back of the sulky and was off to Gulargambone, around 450 kilometres away. It was not only the trainers and jockeys who had to be tough; the horses had to be strong too.

Dries rode a number of winners during his career, and won races such as the Narrabri Cup and Tamworth Newmarket. His greatest feat was to ride the six-horse program at a meeting in Moree during the 1920s.

Like many other riders before him, at the conclusion of his riding career, Dries took up training. Nyperway was his best horse, winning 25 races and picking up some important country silverware, including the 1977 Gunnedah Lightning, the 1978 Inverell Cup and the Moree Newmarket.

BESLEY MURRAY

The story of Besley Murray began down around Balranald in south-western New South Wales, where he spent most of his life. Murray was born at Swan Hill on 22 October 1928 but was taken to Balranald as a baby. Like other Aboriginal children, Murray was refused entry into the local school. His family fought the issue and some years later he was allowed to attend. But he left school early at the age of 13 after he met the manager of Yanga Station, who asked him whether he would like to learn to ride a racehorse. He was only 6 stone (38 kilograms) at the time, and decided to give it a go. Murray was always mad on horses.

'It was the only mode of transport then, there weren't too many cars around,' he said.

Murray was resolute in his view that Aboriginal people do hold a strong affinity with not just the horse but all animals:

> I don't know what it is really, It's just something that they like and can do. I've seen lots of them with horses; it was easier to get a horse than a car. I think that's what it was all about. You'd see lots of little kids. Aboriginal kids three and four of them on a horse riding bareback.

Murray established a reputation as a good horse breaker at an early age. People would come out to get him to break in a difficult horse and he would spend two days over the weekend doing it. In the early days, when he was still attending school, he would ride home in the dark on Sunday night and swim his horse across the Murrumbidgee River.

At one time, he was breaking some horses for a man called Mr McGinley. He used to row a boat across the Murrumbidgee, walk about a mile and work the man's three horses. After about three months of this without pay, he finally built up enough courage to ask for some money for the work.

'Mr McGinley, I was wondering if I could get some money off you for work?'

The man looked down at him.

'Christ, boy, you've been getting the experience for nothing.'

Murray's big start as a jockey occurred when he rode a little mare called Bonny Dawn to victory in the last hurdle race in Balranald in 1943. He was about 15 years old at the time. For Murray, being a jockey was like anything else in life: he needed a good start or a lucky break, and for him that meant good horses. Good horses make good jockeys — they give the jockey a name. Murray was riding half-broken-in things and buckjumpers. And riding in the bush in the 1940s was no picnic. He rode through dust storms and galloped over and around rabbit burrows at the old racecourse. He didn't win a lot of races, but he got a lot of enjoyment out of it.

Murray rode until 1946, when his career as a jockey ended with increasing weight problems, then he went on to ride in Thorpe McConnville's Wild Australia Show. Later he worked on Yanga Station, where he rose to be second in charge of the biggest freehold property in the Southern Hemisphere. He is highly respected member of the local community, and has judged whip-cracking events at the Royal Easter Show in Sydney and been a guest at the Calgary Stampede in Canada.

Murray has witnessed significant social change during his time as a jockey and working around horses. In his early years, things were very tough for Aboriginal people. While he was travelling with McConnville's show, he observed and experienced at first hand the racism and prejudice present in the country. Aboriginal people were not allowed into hotels and picture theatres. One very hot and dry day in Queensland, Murray walked into a hotel for a cold lemon squash but was refused. As he walked back to the show, he ran into two other Aboriginal riders also on their way back to the big top. They were really hostile about their treatment, having been refused a haircut.

Murray's uncle, Freddy Murray, is the subject of much rumour and legend. Members of the family carry the story of him having ridden in England in the early decades of the twentieth century, and having worn the King's colours. Commenting on the story, Murray recalled:

> Yeah, he was a man that started out as a jockey, later he was a great bareback rider. I know that he did ride overseas. It was long before my time and I did hear the stories about him, but I do not have any proof of that sort of thing, and I don't like commenting too much on people and things without any proof. But I believe what I've heard from horse trainers around Balranald that he was a great horseman.

Adding further evidence to the theory of a hidden Aboriginal presence on Australian racecourses, he said, 'There were a lot more Aboriginal people that took part in racing but we never heard of them, they were in the background.' In conclusion, Besley said he felt confident about the future:

> Let's work together and share the best country in the world … the young Aboriginal people today — there is just so much talent out there and I am proud of them, and the thing I dislike the most are the people that put young Aboriginal people down.

Murray is now semi-retired, but is still associated with the people on Yanga Station. He is also coordinator and Aboriginal sites officer for his region.

STAN JOHNSON

Stan Johnson had his first ride in 1939, and was the first of four Aboriginal apprentices linked with Newcastle trainer Keith Tinson. His two brothers, Lin and Dick Johnson, were famed Rugby League players who represented New South Wales.

STAN JOHNSON AND HIS THREE SONS, PHILLIP, WAYNE AND DARRYL. COURTESY NICOLE CLAVERIE FAMILY COLLECTION.

Denali was one of the best horses Stan Johnson ever rode. He won four races on him when Denali was a 2-year-old, before he had made it to the top as a racehorse.

The best wins in Stan Johnson's career included the Northern Stakes at Newcastle and the South Grafton Cup. He also won a lot of country cups around the Tamworth area.

Johnson's career received a severe setback, and almost ended, when he was involved in a car accident. He suffered severe injuries in the crash, but recovered to return to the track.

Stan Johnson's three sons — Phillip, Wayne and Darryl — followed him on to the racetrack and into careers as jockeys. One Saturday afternoon at the 1972 Gunnedah Cup meeting, Johnson and all three of his sons contested the same race, the Ray Kelly Memorial Improvers Handicap. Unfortunately, none of the Johnsons was successful. Rather, it was another Aboriginal jockey — Merv Maynard, on Hard Lad — who won the event.

But the Johnsons were not altogether out of the limelight that day, as Stan took out the Maiden on Richmond River, starting at 10/1, and Phillip punched home Scully Park in the 1200 metres Consolation Improvers Handicap, starting at 8/1.

Stan Johnson's career endured into the 1970s. He remains, and is remembered as, a top rider — especially in the Tamworth area, to which he returned to ride and live in the 1960s and 1970s.

KENNY BRODERICK

Kenny Broderick was born in April 1930. During the Second World War, at the age of 14, he was indentured as an apprentice jockey to Pompey Conquest in Brisbane. He did not get on with Conquest, which made his life in the stables very difficult. He suffered from discrimination and was starved of riding opportunities. After two and a half years, he gained a release from Conquest and moved on to the stables of Roley Wall, where he continued to battle without ever being given a real go, but still managed to ride a number of winners in the Queensland country area. It was a tough period for the young jockey, and the difficulties he faced were hard to understand, as some felt he had a natural gift and a great seat in the saddle.

Denied opportunity was responsible for forcing him away from racing, and he took to the boxing ring. In 1947–48, he was crowned Queensland Golden Gloves Boxing Champion. Kenny Broderick was married and raised children in Brisbane. He died a young man in the early 1980s.

KENNY BRODERICK ON THE JOB IN THE 1940S. COURTESY EILEEN RALLAH.

BARRY HAGAN

Barry Hagan was an Aboriginal rider from Brewarrina. He left home at an early age and moved to Queensland in search of a career as a jockey. The family lost track of him, but he rode winners up around Rockhampton and Gympie.

FRANK AND JACK DUVAL

Frank and Jack Duval were both exceptional and accomplished horsemen, who made their mark on international racing. It has been said that they rode all their lives and they rode everywhere.

Although family members assumed that they were of Maori descent, family history research and oral stories later established that they were in fact Aboriginal. Undoubtedly fear played a part in them denying or not knowing their Aboriginal identity.

'If the locals had known we had anything to do with or concerned with Aborigines we would not have got any assistance,' Frank said.

James Bardon, described as 'one of the most notable men on the turf', once described Frank Duval as 'the best cross-country rider in Australia'. Duval was also an accomplished horseman in the show ring. Horses went well for him over hurdles, and he became adept at getting them over high jumps. He was on a horse

that cleared 7 feet 4 inches (almost 2.25 metres) at Quirindi — at that time a record for a high jump in Australia and still talked about generations later.

Frank Duval weighed 6 stone (38.1 kilograms) and was only 12 years old when he began his racing career with the late Frank McGrath in Sydney. In the early part of the twentieth century, boys were still allowed to ride at a young age. Frank Duval's most important win as a jockey was in the Rosehill Guineas on Wahaweta. He stayed with McGrath for seven years, learning the art of race riding as well as the rudiments of racehorse training. He remarked years later that it was then that he 'decided to get about a bit'.

His wanderlust first took him to India and then Africa, where he was associated with his brother, Jack. Jack Duval had established himself as a rider overseas, especially in Asia. He never returned to Australia, remaining in South-East Asia until he died. He is buried at Ocean Beach Cemetery in Kuala Lumpur in Malaysia.

At the time Frank Duval ventured overseas, Jack had retired as a rider and was training big teams of horses. Frank and his brother proved a successful combination. Frank won a Penang Cup on a horse called Silver Hampton, and he also won important races in South Africa. He rode in India for four years and in Africa for two. Elder brother Jack trained for several Maharajahs in India and Frank Duval got to know them very well. He found them good patrons — generous and considerate.

On his return to Australia, increased weight problems saw Frank's riding career come to a close. He took up training back up in the Walcha area. Carew was the best horse he trained. Merv Maynard rode him, winning two races.

'Yeah I rode for Frank. Carew, I remember him — he was a very quick horse. Old Frank came down here from nowhere. He was a neat and dapper little fella. I didn't know him from a bar of soap … I knew Frank was Aboriginal just on his looks. Not that anything was ever said. In those days you never heard anything about Aboriginal jockeys … Yeah it was all hidden,' Maynard recalled.

DOUG HODGSON

Douglas Hodgson was born in 1938 at Marree in South Australia. He was the eldest son of Charles Hodgson, an English settler, and Myra (formerly Hull) from the Southern Aranda and Arabunna people of northern South Australia.

DOUG HODGSON GREETS THE JUDGE FIRST IN ONE OF HIS MANY BUSH VICTORIES. COURTESY HODGSON FAMILY COLLECTION.

One of 11 children, he started working with livestock from a young age, having horses and camels to look after in a paddock close to the old Alice Springs racecourse. Doug was responsible for the care of the animals from before daybreak, and then again in the late afternoon after school. He gained part-time work at the local store at the Alice Springs Gap, where he used to serve Albert Namatjira, the famous Indigenous painter.

His father recognised his capacity to work with horses at an early stage, when he was riding without a saddle or any formal training. A career as a jockey was a logical choice, even though a young Doug had to leave his family in the Northern Territory to pursue his dreams.

Leaving home at the age of 14 was incredibly tough for someone so young, making the journey from Alice Springs to Adelaide by the famous Ghan Train without any family support.

He started his apprenticeship as a jockey in 1952, coming out of his time in 1959. During his apprenticeship, he spent time in Adelaide with Ron Brody, and later with Quorn and Port Augusta trainers. He rode on all three metropolitan Adelaide tracks, and at many regional South Australian towns and Alice Springs race meetings.

During his apprenticeship, Charlie Stevens, well-known steeplechase jockey from the 1950s, had followed Doug's career with interest, and said in the *Centralian Advocate*, 'He sits nicely and handles a horse very well indeed — a few years and he should go places.'

On one occasion at the Port Augusta Racing Club meeting, Doug rode the card, winning every race at the meeting. This was a rare occurrence and a career high point. His young sisters were proud of their older brother, and they can remember going to Alice Springs to watch him race, sitting in the grandstand.

Doug was a film extra as a jockey in the international 1950s movie *The Sundowners*, which was shot locally in the Flinders Ranges with international stars Robert Mitchum, Peter Ustinov and Deborah Kerr.

Between 1956 and 1959, Doug rode 68 winners. Family members were unable to find out Doug's total career winning rides because a fire at the South Australian Jockey Club destroyed the race records. His career commenced in 1952 and finished in 1959, and the family estimates that he would have had up to 200 wins at various regional racetracks, including Alice Springs, Jamestown, Marree, Whyalla, Quorn, Strathalbyn and Port Augusta, to name just a few.

Leon Macdonald, a highly respected horseman and best known as the trainer of Southern Speed, the winner of the 2011 Caulfield Cup, remembers Doug as 'a very good rider, probably a bit heavy to be a competitive metropolitan rider but as a bush rider he was probably as good as there was … Doug rode a lot of winners.' For a short period, Doug lived with the Macdonald family in Port Augusta.

Doug retired from race riding in 1959, as he and his wife Shirley were due to have their first child and he needed a reliable income to support them. He also had an ongoing struggle keeping his weight down to the required levels for a jockey.

In his retirement, Doug kept his hand in the horse racing industry as a keen volunteer by being the head judge at the local Port Augusta Trotting Club. Doug's great-grand-daughter, Jayde, is also a very talented rider, and no doubt has inherited some of Doug's passion, skills and ability. Doug died on 8 November 2004 at the age of 66.

This information was provided by Ian Hodgson and the descendants of Doug Hodgson.

GORDON TAYLOR

GORDON TAYLOR WINS AN APPRENTICE RACE ON ROYAL BLOOM FOR GRISDALE; PICTURED HERE WITH GRISDALE AND TINSON. COURTESY OF THE *NEWCASTLE MORNING HERALD*.

When Gordon Taylor was 14, his dad told him to get out and get himself a job. There were 12 in the family and his father worked as a boundary rider. So there was nothing for him at home.

Taylor began his apprenticeship in the bush, but had his indentures transferred to Keith Tinson in 1955. He arrived in Newcastle by train and was picked up at the station by Merv and Judy Maynard, accompanied by their baby son. Taylor had spent 12 months with Harold Davidson before he joined Keith Tinson, who was a hard boss. One time Taylor had a boil on his leg that became infected and blew up into a huge mass. Tinson's attitude was that he could still get out of bed and do the 26 horses with which he had to ride work.

Merv Maynard was the leading rider then. When he came down to the track, he always called around to the stables and looked into the room to see how Taylor was going. This time he looked at Taylor's leg and just told him to get back into bed. He would ride the horses. He did the same again when an abscess meant that all Taylor's teeth had to be taken out.

In November 1960, both Taylor and Merv Maynard were suspended from riding. They spent Melbourne Cup Day out on Lake Macquarie fishing, and listened to Hi-Jinx winning the Cup on the radio.

When he had given up riding and had taken on training, Darby Munro offered Tinson good money for Taylor's indentures, but Tinson wouldn't let Taylor go.

Taylor was regularly called a 'black bastard' out on the track, but mostly it was just people talking through an empty pocket if the jockey had been beaten on a horse on which they had put their money. One time he won a double at Newcastle then missed the kick in the next and was beaten in a photo finish. As he came on to the track for the next race, a punter was there waiting on the fence.

'Don't fall asleep this time you black mug.'

'Of course he fell asleep. He's been up with your missus all night,' the following rider quipped.

Gordon's younger brother, Dennis, also ventured into the racing world and was apprenticed to famed Hunter Valley horseman Danny Edwards before weight troubles forced him to abandon his dream of becoming a jockey.

For Gordon Taylor, racing was a great preparation for life. If you could survive in racing, you could overcome anything.

JIMMY LESLIE

Jimmy Leslie was another Aboriginal country boy who ventured to the 'Big Smoke' (Sydney) during the 1960s. He rode winners for Tommy Smith and also rode for many of the other big stables at the time. He later returned to the Gunnedah and Tamworth area, where he continued to ride successfully for a number of years. He is well remembered as a 'brilliant little horseman'.

HARRY FULLER

Harry Fuller was from Warren in Western New South Wales, and is recognised in the *Guinness Book of Records* as having won the most races on the same horse, Grey Ghost. John Dries recalled that, 'Dad always tried to put Harry on if he took a horse out west ... One of the tidiest jockeys you'd ever see.'

Norm Rose revealed the banter and camaraderie that existed between Aboriginal jockeys, 'Harry Fuller was a real card ... I used to go out there to Dubbo and he'd always have a go at me. Call me the blackfella from Newcastle and he was the blackfella from out there. "What are you doin' out here in my country brother?", all that sort of stuff.'

BILL O'BRIEN

Bill O'Brien was an accomplished jockey from the Mid-North Coast of New South Wales. His career started in Sydney at the age of 15 when he was apprenticed to Fred Hood at Rosehill. But he returned home to Port Macquarie and established himself as one of the top local riders. He retired in 1986, having won the Port Macquarie Cup in 1972, the Grafton Country Cup, the Gladstone Cup twice and the Christmas Cup in Lismore. He also rode a winner in Brisbane against some of the leading riders of the day.

'I teamed up with a trainer called Glen Hodge and we had a very successful period over many years,' he said.

In 2008, Bill O'Brien was named Hastings Citizen of the Year for his work promoting cultural awareness and advocacy of Indigenous issues. As a Birpai elder, the former jockey conducts bush tucker tours at Sea Acres Nature Reserve in Port Macquarie, the traditional land of his people.

He said that, traditionally, 'It was a piece of paradise for Aboriginal people with everything from nuts, berries and honey to bush turkeys, possums even flying foxes, native palms were used by early settlers for water diversion and the fronds of the palm by his Aboriginal people to wrap and cook the flying foxes in.'

He says the coastal people, known as the Morning Star people, were very lucky because their diet consisted of seafood and they made fish traps with rocks and the tide as a method of catching fish.

DAVID MATHEWS

David Mathews grew up on Caroona Mission (originally Walhollow Station), located about 20 kilometres from Quirindi in northern New South Wales. Caroona was established as an Aboriginal mission in the late 1870s. There were usually around 200 Aboriginal people living at the mission under the control of the Protection Board manager. The station was a significant distance from Quirindi and all the facilities, such as a school, church and a hall, reflect a people living an institutional existence in an isolated place.

As a young boy, Mathews was given opportunities to drove sheep for Mick Barnett.

'I was 12 or 13 and knocked around looking after sheep,' he said.

Through that experience, he gained a position on Mr Jim Trail's sheep and cattle stations, where his job was to look after the merino stud rams. David held dreams of becoming a jockey and his heroes were Neville Sellwood and Tulloch. Around 1965, a visitor to the property asked whether he would be interested in becoming a jockey. The visitor had connections with horse trainer Norm Collins at Cessnock, and he contacted the trainer on Mathews' behalf.

Mathews recalled: 'Here I am up in the back of beyond and the mail truck only comes out once a week.' David received a letter from the trainer stating that if he was interested, then there was an opportunity to come down and start an apprenticeship. David read the letter and was ecstatic: 'I jumped over the moon thinking that someone is interested in giving me a go.'

He raced straight down to the boss's house in the dark to inform him of the news. It may have been a slight misjudgement, as the boss called back: 'I could

A YOUNG DAVID MATTHEWS UNSADDLING AFTER A WIN. TRAINER NORM COLLINS IS IN THE BACKGROUND. COURTESY DAVID MATTHEWS.

have shot you in the dark.' But the boss relented and said, 'It is up to you. If you want to go I wont stop you.'

Young David could not sleep all night with excitement. The mail truck was due to go back into Quirindi the next day, and he was packed and ready to jump on board. He went back into Quirindi and informed his mother that he had been offered an apprenticeship as a jockey. His mother replied, 'You will have to ask your father.' So David trekked out to another property where his father was working, only to be told to ask his mother. Mathews stated, 'I was sick of the to and fro to and fro, and I said to mum, "Well, I'm going."' She called after him, 'You'll be back with your tail between your legs and crying.' David looked back and said, 'At least I am going to have a go.'

He boarded the train at Quirindi and journeyed down to Newcastle. When he arrived at Broadmeadow station — 'the biggest station I had ever seen with those big stairs that went up to the high level bridge' — Mathews saw a bandy-legged man walking towards him on the platform — it was Norm Collins, who had parked his car over the road. When David got into the car, the trainer looked him up and down and said, 'Our first stop will be the barbers.' David had long hair and was almost ready to jump out of the car. On the drive back to Cessnock, the trainer asked David about himself and his riding experience. After his haircut, he met the Collins family and settled into the life of an apprentice jockey. He received 'three feeds a day and it was like feeding a parrot. I was getting two pound ten a week and my washing and ironing done.' Six months after arriving, he had his first barrier trial and it went quite well; soon afterwards, he had another three or four jumps from the barrier.

He never won any premierships or big cup races, but he booted home a good few winners before Mother Nature stepped in and stopped his career with weight problems: 'I had to look after my weight from the jump. I spent a lot of time in the sauna and popping pills to reduce weight.'

Regal Problem was the best horse David rode during his career, and — somewhat appropriately for an Aboriginal rider — he took out the Captain Cook Flying on the horse at Broadmeadow:

> *Racegoers were amazed at her performance in carrying 9 stone 4 pounds [59 kilograms] over the strenuous 6 furlongs [1200 metres] at Newcastle, and began to applaud when it was apparent the mare would win. The clapping continued until the mare well ridden by apprentice David Mathews returned to scale … When Starlon ridden by 'The Professor', Jack Thompson, made its bid after straightening*

up, many racegoers thought Regal Problem would tire because of her big weight. When Mathews gave her rein, she drew away to score by two and a half lengths from Starlon.

Miss Ketch was a very smart sprinter ridden by David, and she broke the Australasian record in 1968. He was on her back in Sydney when she came in third behind Wenona Girl and Skyhigh. David was the leading Newcastle apprentice for a couple of seasons.

In 1970, due to the continuing weight problems, he walked off the course and straight into David Williams' Newcastle blacksmith shop. He spent 16 enjoyable years as a blacksmith until back problems forced his retirement from that industry.

David had no regrets. For a time he took out a trainer's licence — more as a hobby than anything else. He also worked in the local timber yard and, wanting to put back into the local Aboriginal community, he worked for Yarnteen and the Awabakal Co-op in youth services. He gained all of his qualifications and fostered two young disabled Aboriginal brothers, for whom he and second wife Wendy have provided a loving family environment. Wendy is the daughter of former top Newcastle jockey Peter Burnett. On looking back, David Mathews has had a roller-coaster ride through his riding life, but he has enjoyed his time at the track.

MERV MARION

Merv Marion was a top-class rider in Queensland before a serious fall at the Gold Coast in 1985 curtailed his career. As a stark reminder of the brutal nature of the sport, he suffered brain damage as a result of the fall when his mount, Stolen Cash, rolled on top of him. He survived on life support for a long period before his death.

REG 'PUNTER' HART

Reg 'Punter' Hart always had a pony. His father was a top-class horse breaker and stockman, and a good teacher. Reg's father was taken from his Aboriginal family as a baby back in 1885. He was taken in by the Hart family at Charleville, and became a drover and a top-notch buckjump rider. When he was little, Reg would climb a tree up to the first fork so he could get on a horse.

'My old dad gave me some pretty good advice early on. He said, "Son, keep your eyes and ears open and your mouth shut", and I've pretty much followed his philosophy throughout my life and it stood me in good stead. I'm just sorry that he didn't see what I achieved.'

Hart learned to stand on his own two feet, and his father made sure he stayed at school until he was 15. He achieved very good results at school, and was always near the top of the class. He learnt shorthand, typing and bookkeeping. However, he quickly realised that, despite high academic achievement, there was no way in the world in those days that a coloured bloke could get a job in an office or a shop. He really wanted to be an accountant, but that was just not possible.

Hart was born in 1915, and began his racing life as a bush jockey out around Charleville. He was a quick learner and was riding trackwork before he had left school. By the time he was 16, he was riding in races and from that point in time he was always tied up with racehorses. Hart rode between Charleville, Augathella and Cunnamulla. There was a lot to be learnt from riding in the bush.

'It is still best to keep young riders out in the bush until they have learnt the ropes. Those old bush jockeys, they were men not boys. You learnt the tricks of the trade quick … If you rode two bad races they would crucify you,' he said.

Denied working and riding opportunities during the Depression forced Hart to go bush, so he headed up into the Northern Territory, droving. By the time he was 21, he was a boss drover. At the end of the Second World War, Hart moved to Brisbane with his wife and three daughters, looking for better opportunities. He had no job, no home and only £20 in his pocket.

He worked on the wharf, was a wardsman at the hospital, worked for the local council on the roads and spent time in a bakery. While working at the bakery, he operated the SP (starting price off-course bookmakers) for the baker. He ran the book and was always one step ahead of the police, and was never convicted.

But the pull of the racecourse was eventually too strong, and Hart returned to the track, working for George Boland. He had kept his hand in over the years and had trained a number of horses.

'When I joined up with George we won money everywhere. I wondered how long is this going to go on for.'

Boland trained Galleon King, which won the Brisbane Cup in 1969 — Hart backed him at 66/1. During this period, the Boland stable had a lot of good horses. Hart's early background as a bush jockey had equipped him well: he was very horse- and street-wise. He held the position as stable foreman, and his astute knowledge was instrumental in his punting success. Hart loved the track and the characters of racing, and he went on to become one of the most recognised and familiar faces on Brisbane racetracks.

WILLIAM LORD

William Lord has the distinction of having had his first race ride at Randwick during the early 1940s, and winning the event.

He began his riding career when a friend of the family put him in touch with Sydney trainer Mick Polson. Lord's father was only a 'little fella', and a few of his uncles were bush jockeys — not outstanding riders, just good bush horsemen.

Working in a racing stable was hard in those early days. Mick Polson was not an easy person for whom to work, and Lord didn't get on well with him. Polson's apprentice jockeys had to get up early — at 3 am — muck out boxes and take the horses to the racecourse. They worked them, then brought them home and cleaned them. The days were long: from 3.30 am until 7 pm, seven days a week — with only one day off a fortnight.

But Polson had a good team of horses in his stable. He had taken champion miler Winooka to America during the Depression years. Magnificent was another outstanding individual — a beautiful horse, a big chestnut by Ajax with three white feet and a white blaze. He won the Breeders Plate, Sires Produce, Champagne Stakes, AJC Derby and VRC Derby. Lord broke him in and was his strapper, and was supposed to ride him in the Breeders Plate but unfortunately had not had the compulsory 10 rides for an apprentice jockey.

Like many other jockeys, Lord developed weight troubles. He became too heavy for Sydney and so moved to Newcastle. He had friends up there, including Stan Johnson, Eric Middleton, Jimmy Tinson and Billy Wade.

But the weight battle did not end in Newcastle, and Lord had a tough tussle to keep his weight down. He started training at Tom Maguire's Newcastle gym to take off weight, training and boxing with the Sands boys, the famed boxing family from Kempsey. Eventually he had to concede he was fighting a losing battle and he gave riding away, deciding to give boxing a go. He fought for about two years, fighting a draw with Jimmy Reeves in the New South Wales State Lightweight Title in Sydney.

Lord may not have had a long riding career, but very few riders could boast of riding a winner at Randwick on their first race ride and going on to perform very well as a professional boxer.

GEOFF BOOTH

Geoff Booth was a top rider up around Rockhampton, who showed that he could mix it with the best of them whenever he ventured south. In 1998 he captured the Country Cup at Eagle Farm on Rash Account. He won a number of races in

Brisbane and had two stints riding in Melbourne during the 1980s. Booth was destined to be a stockman until a teacher at Woorabinda saw him out mustering cattle at the age of 8 and suggested he should try to become a jockey instead, because of his small build.

Booth's first winner was in a two-horse race at Callaghan Park, and it gave him a tremendous thrill. As a 17-year-old, he won on crack 3-year-old Minto Crag at Eagle Farm.

In a similar move to that initiated by Darby McCarthy, with his Aboriginal apprentice school, Booth organised a Commonwealth government-backed riding school for Aboriginal boys in Rockhampton. The scheme sadly faltered when funding stopped. Booth is quietly spoken but articulate and forthright, and he is passionate in his belief that Aboriginal kids provide an untapped reservoir of riding talent in Queensland:

> There's a lot of kids in the communities right through the north and west who have great natural ability. Just about everyone has a horse and many of the kids are small enough to become jockeys. But a lot of them are taking up bull-riding to follow the rodeo circuit. They need someone to go out there and talk to them about racing and identify the kids with the right ability, size and temperament. It's important to talk to them in their environment where they're comfortable … discipline is the thing if a youngster is going to succeed, and racing is a tough game. That's why temperament is important. I'd be looking for kids who are prepared for the long haul. Racing has been good to me and I want to put something back into the industry.

GLEN PICKWICK

Glen Pickwick was one of a number of young Aboriginal riders who broke through into city racing during the 1980s. An accomplished horseman, he proved he had the ability to match it in the top grade, but suffered from unfair and constant media comparisons with Darby McCarthy.

Pickwick came from Queensland and began his apprenticeship with Neil Strong at Eagle Farm in Brisbane. He enjoyed his first win at 16 on a horse named Empan. The 10-year-old horse cleared out to win by two-and-a-half lengths in an open handicap at Wondai on 30 May 1981.

Unfortunately, after his initial success Pickwick broke his collarbone in a fall from an unraced 2-year-old at Albion Park and lost six weeks of racing. After only a week back, a fall from a bicycle broke the bone again and he had to spend another

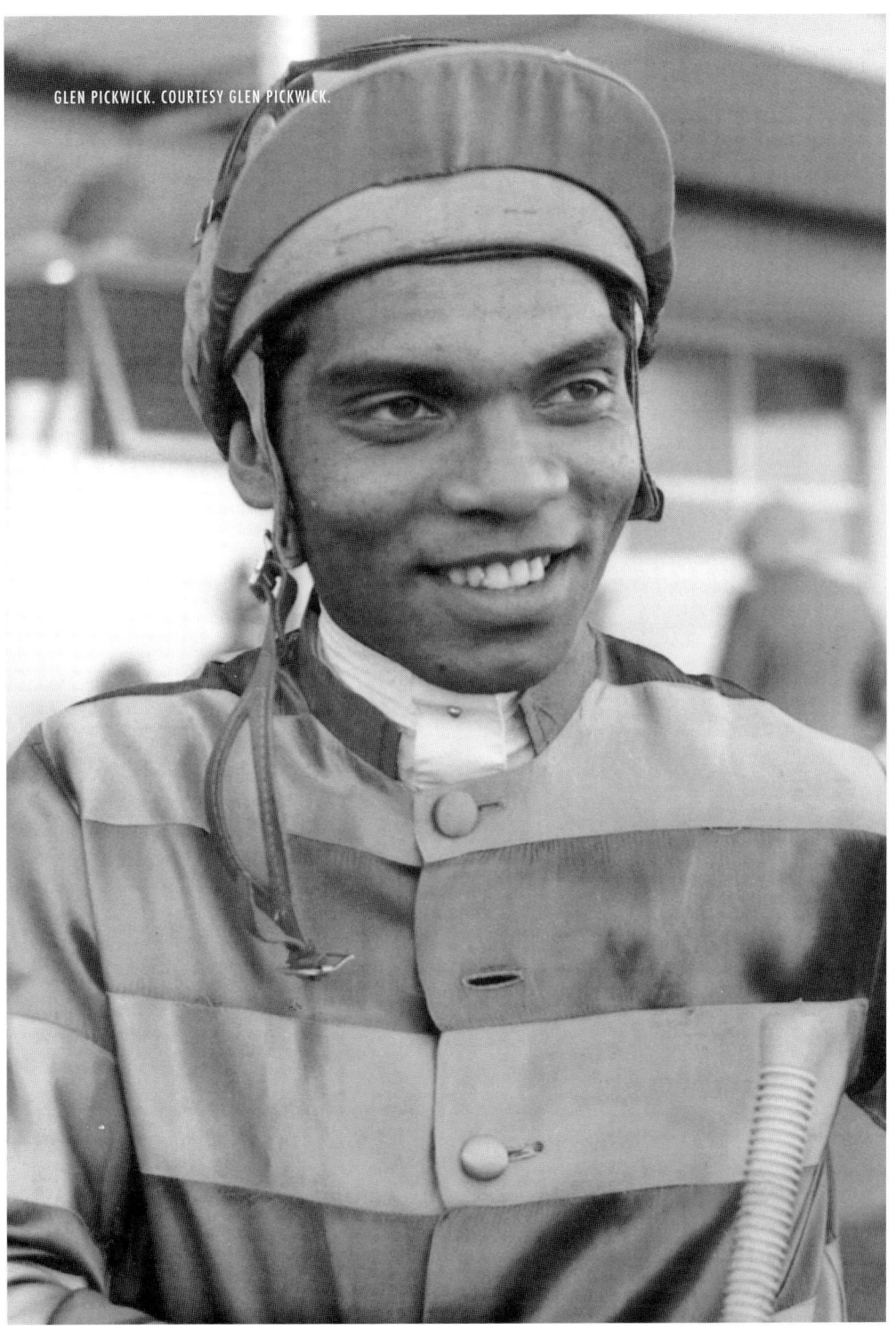

GLEN PICKWICK. COURTESY GLEN PICKWICK.

eight weeks convalescing. Neil Strong advised Pickwick to look for an alternative stable. Ros Ellwood at Grafton gave him a chance.

In his first year, Pickwick rode 27 winners, mostly in southern Queensland and the Northern Rivers region of New South Wales. He showed that he had promise and talent. Glenn Innes trainer Clive Dixon gave him a ride on 6-year-old gelding Amaretto in the Lismore Cup; starting at 16/1, the horse cleared out to beat veteran campaigner Neared by three-quarters of a length.

Pickwick's talent had not gone unnoticed, and only three weeks after his victory in the Lismore Cup, he and another Northern Rivers apprentice were allowed to spend time in Sydney with one of Australia's leading trainers, Neville Begg. Begg was impressed by Pickwick's skill and offered him a three-month trial in Sydney.

'He's a boy of the future — a rider of great natural balance ... he's strong, especially around the shoulders and arms. He just might make the grade,' Begg said.

At his first race meeting in Sydney, Pickwick booted home Lord of Persia for Neville Begg at Warwick Farm. Under hard riding, Lord of Persia held off all challengers in the last race of the day. It was a great start, and Pickwick proved himself to be very capable. He rode his last metropolitan winner in 1993. Despondent with limited opportunities, at one point he gave the game away. But he decided at the age of 37 to give it one more go, after being offered a good ride at Bathurst. He shed 5 kilograms in as many days to take the ride and win the race. In early 2002, he won the Glen Innes Cup on board veteran galloper Darahim.

LYALL APPO

Lyall Appo – like his brother Bradley Appo (see below) — was a Wakka Wakka man. He overcame an impoverished and difficult start to his life to establish a riding career. Both Lyall's parents worked on cattle stations around Queensland – his father Lionel as a stockman and his mother Yvonne doing domestic duties. Together, Lionel and Yvonne had nine children, with Lyall being the oldest. Lyall explained why he decided to be a jockey:

> I come from a generation of stockman and grew up on property. That's where I learned to ride — on stations. All my life we were brought up as ringers (cattle station workers), and every kid was taught from our uncles how to ride.
>
> Because I'm a little fella, my uncles had always told me that I would make a good jockey. Being in the country, there were always race meetings on and all of my uncles would ride in stockmen's races, so one thing I always wanted to be was a jockey.'

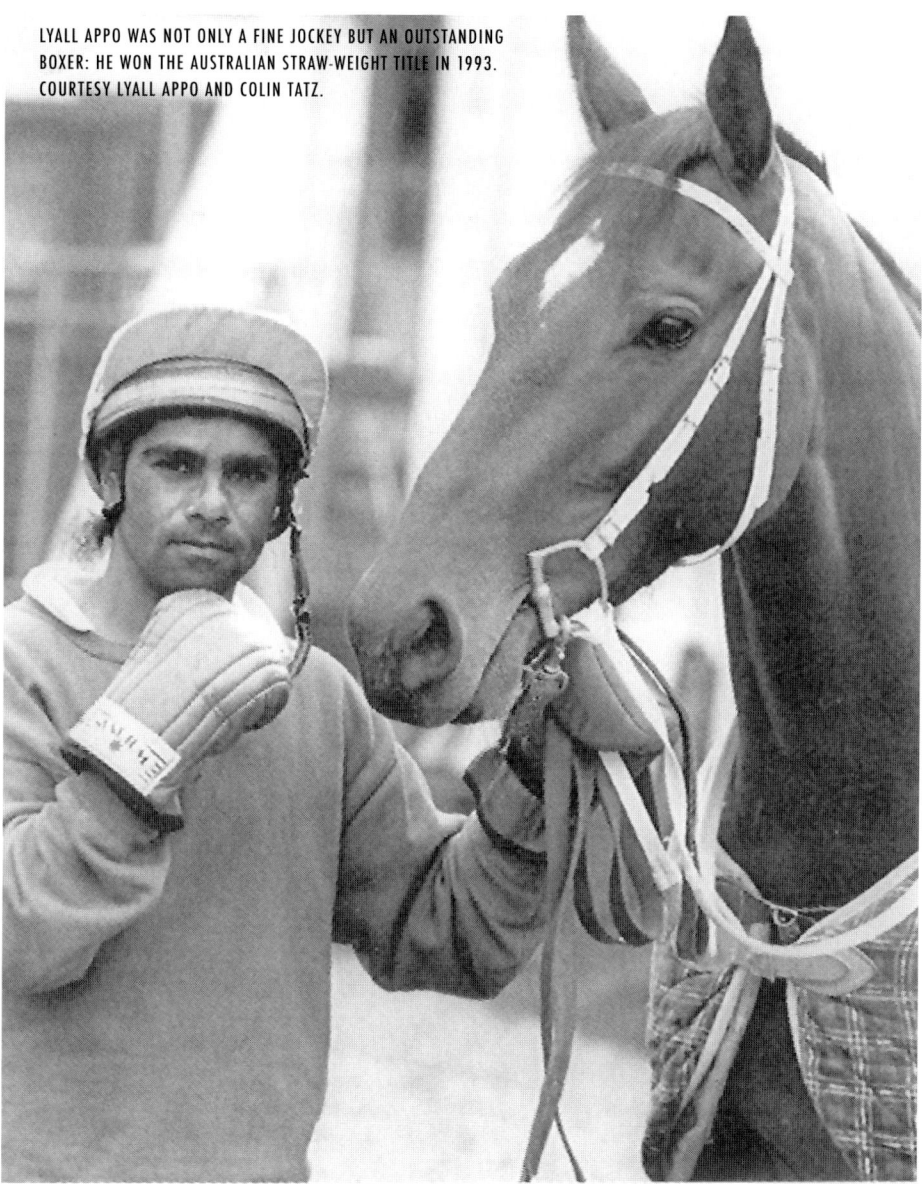

LYALL APPO WAS NOT ONLY A FINE JOCKEY BUT AN OUTSTANDING BOXER: HE WON THE AUSTRALIAN STRAW-WEIGHT TITLE IN 1993. COURTESY LYALL APPO AND COLIN TATZ.

The Appo brothers (Bradley is two years younger than Lyall) grew up in the small town of Eidsvold in central Queensland, where Aboriginal people were just being allowed to move back into town. It was only a little Aboriginal community but it was very close. As they moved into town, a lot of things went wrong. In some cases, alcohol took over and Aboriginal families, their structure, identity, brothers and sisters, kinship just fell apart. Then the white part of it — the government

LYALL APPO. COURTESY LYALL APPO.

— came in. The Appo brothers were the first children in that community to be taken away from their parents. It was a major disruption to their young lives, and it continued like that for a few years — being taken away and then getting back home again.

Lyall left Eidsvold to begin his life as an apprentice jockey at the age of 15 under the guidance of Toowoomba trainer Bruce Cameron, the father-in-law of well-known retired Toowoomba jockey Mick Aspinall.

'I had a six-year apprenticeship — in fact, I was in the last batch of apprentices that went through a six-year apprenticeship. It changed to five years after that,' he said.

While not keeping a tally of his career winners to date, Lyall had a 'successful apprenticeship'; he recalled, 'I was always up with the leading apprentices most of the time. I outrode my claim in Toowoomba and almost outrode my city claim while I was still an apprentice.'

He rode his first two winners on a 4-year-old called Rio Dell, a mare that had been born and bred in his old home town. The victories gave Lyall a great boost, and he quickly rode doubles and trebles in a career that eventually led him to Brisbane.

Despite his success on the track, Lyall quickly realised that the life of an apprentice jockey was not easy. The experience was similar to his six years being fostered out with white families. He felt like a prisoner trapped in a system from which he thought he had escaped. Young jockeys were more or less slaves. But really racing was a level playing field for black and white jockeys:

> To compete and ride against these fellas and achieve and ride winners at metropolitan tracks is the pinnacle of a level playing field — there the racism does not exist. It exists outside of that jockeys' room which is society but you just have to stay strong enough to overcome that.

Lyall had the spirit to have a go, and was imbued with a strong drive to achieve. He never regretted his decision to become a jockey. He learnt how to respect people and to earn that respect for himself. He was a top rider in Brisbane during the 1980s, and was regarded as one of the top apprentices of his time. He won races such as the Metropolitan Exhibition Handicap, QTC Tattersals Plate and Rockhampton Newmarket.

Lyall rode against some of the great names of the Australian turf during his time in the saddle, including Mick Dittman, Peter Cook, Ron Quinton, Roy Higgins, Harry White, Jim Cassidy and Malcolm Johnston. They were great jockeys, but Lyall realised they were not the same colour as him. The only role models and inspiration he had through his young life were Evonne Goolagong, Lionel Rose and Darby McCarthy.

Lyall, who said he'd ridden 'heaps of winners at Eagle Farm and Doomben', also had a couple of stints riding in Sydney:

> I went down there on loan to [then] successful Warwick Farm-based trainer John Rosenthal. I had a couple of stints in Sydney throughout my apprenticeship and was lucky enough to ride at all the tracks in and around Sydney and I rode placegetters at Randwick, Gosford and Hawkesbury. But I'm a Queenslander born and bred, and I always enjoyed coming back here.

On his first visit to Randwick when he was only 16 years of age, everyone in the jockeys' room kept calling him Glen. They thought he was Glen Pickwick.

'Glen and I are rather similar, but I reckon I am a lot better looking than him,' Lyall joked.

At Randwick, he sat down next to Malcolm Johnston and was quickly accepted and treated as an equal:

> That's the type of blokes they were. It was just respect that made you feel a part of that community and that life. It is the same thing if I see a little Aboriginal kid, a Murri rider, come into the room. I just say, 'Hey brother come over here, your alright here brus?' These fellas aren't any different to us. You will be alright, it's a family.

Lyall is very forthright about his Aboriginality and his identity:

> There was a lot of racism in racing when I started. It's hard, as an Aboriginal kid, to make it in a white dominated sport. There weren't any other Aboriginal identities racing at that time who I could relate to. Now when I see Aboriginal kids that are riding who look up to me, I know why.

Darby McCarthy was his hero, and he idolised him. He would have liked to have had inspiration from Aboriginal heroes as a kid:

> I wished I'd had that when I was 15 because I would have known the reason why they kept calling me Indigenous, and every time they wrote about me they called me Aboriginal. It is because that is what I am. I am what I am. I've had the chance to set records in all sports. The main reason I set those records was because people put me down. They put my colour down. They put me down, if they had said a blackfella couldn't do it. Then I would be in it. If they said a blackfella could not fly the space-shuttle, then I would want to do it. Maybe I'd take Darby McCarthy and Mr Merv Maynard along for the ride just to be sure.

Over the years, he has seen the change in attitude from the people in the stands:

> I get a lot of support from the public now. When I use to go out as a kid, people would be on the fence and they'd be saying, 'Oh, look at the blackfella riding', you know? But now it's, 'Oh, Appo's here'.

Lyall Appo unknowingly followed the path of William Lord 40 years before him when he took on boxing. The jockeys used to have a reputation for being good fighters. Two in particular — Neil Williams and Carl Symons — used to think they were the boxers at the local pub. Someone raised the idea of getting these jockeys who thought they could fight involved in a boxing tournament. But when it came to the day, Neil Williams pulled out with riding commitments in Melbourne.

Grahame Cook recommended Lyall as a replacement and Carl Symons asked whether he was interested. Lyall jumped straight up off his seat in the jockeys' room and responded, snarling, 'Yeah I'll fight you. I'll fight you right now.'

Poor Symons nearly had a heart attack.

'No it's boxing, I don't want to fight you right now.'

Initially Lyall had just thought it was some sort of joke, but they persisted in pressing him about it. Eventually he went home and discussed it with his wife, Michelle, who was none too keen to see her husband climb into the boxing ring. But they would not give up and in the end Lyall agreed. When he arrived on the night of the fight, someone asked whether he could fight.

'I'll be alright,' he replied.

When he climbed into the ring, he was not prepared for the response of the screaming crowd.

'Bash that black bastard, bash him Symons, bash that black thing!'

It was like waving a red rag in front of a bull. Before the fight even started, Lyall walked across the ring and glared at poor Carl Symons.

'I am going to knock you clean out. I am sick to death of all of these people running me down all the time.'

As soon as the bell rang, he rushed across the ring and went 'whoosh'. The fight was supposed to go three rounds, but it only went one-and-a-half. In Lyall's words, he 'punched the pisser out of Carl Symons'.

Lyall realised that night that no matter what he did, he was always going to be nailed as a black person.

Jeff Malcolm, a former top boxer and at the time a trainer, approached Lyall after the fight and asked him who had taught him to fight.

'Who taught me how to fight? All of these white people,' he replied.

Malcolm was impressed with Lyall's natural boxing ability, and asked him to come down and train at his gym. Lyall just got better and better. There were more promotional fights organised and he started to belt up all of the other jockeys. They started bringing fighting jockeys from all over the country and he beat them all.

'I finished up giving away the jockeys because I was belting up all of the people I knew. I hated doing it because they were the same fellas I was riding with,' Lyall said.

Lyall turned to professional boxing and reached its summit when he captured the national straw-weight title.

> I did end up getting a lot of respect for my brothers. I ended up teaching a lot of white people what brother means. Someone would say, 'How come you call him brother?' and I'd say, 'Because he is my brother.' They'd say, 'He's not your brother. He's not your brother at all.' I would finish up replying, 'Yes he is my brother, he is the same in here.' I would point to my heart and that is the difference. All Aboriginal people are related and that is understood.

Initially, and somewhat prematurely, Lyall hung up his saddle. At the time he had few regrets, and he looked back on his years in the saddle as just reward for the gift he had been given:

> I started believing spiritually in myself and my family. It brought out this gift in me, which was fighting. I learnt to box and I learnt to control the

boxing. There was an art in how to control these fists. They had only been used to being a jockey that was all they could do. I had believed that all I could do was control a half ton of animal. I had never had to fight anyone before.

However, in 2001 at the age of 38, the pull of racing was too great and Lyall Appo made a return to the racetrack. He reduced his weight to 52 kilograms and was reissued with his jockey's licence; he was soon riding winners again — and delighted to be back where he belonged.

'I am now settled with my family, my Aboriginal heritage and myself,' he said.

In 2009, racegoers at Caloundra cushion track meeting were treated to a special bit of theatre when Lyall Appo and the despised outsider in Race 3, Elton's Son, shocked all on course and Sky Channel viewers when they gave their rivals a galloping exhibition. There was nothing untoward about a horse giving its rivals a galloping exhibition, except that in this instance the winning partnership of Elton's Son and Lyall Appo paid odds of $69 on the Unitab.

Lyall Appo rarely rides at TAB meetings these days, preferring to focus on the country circuit. In fact, for many years he has been one of the most respected riders on that circuit, generally commanding a full book of rides wherever he chooses to ride on a given Saturday.

Ironically, it was that commitment to the Saturday country circuit riding that gave Lyall the opportunity to ride Elton's Son at Caloundra. He said:

> I rode Elton's Son when he won at Esk in March and last Friday was my seventh consecutive ride on the horse. His last run at Beaudesert was exceptionally good and he really felt good in his last 100 metres that day, giving me the indication that he was looking for further, so I mentioned that to the horse's trainer, John Fahey, and he started looking for a race for him around 1600 or 1800 metres, but this 2150 metre race was the only one John could find.
>
> I said to John before the race that I'd ride him off the speed to give him every opportunity to run the trip, but going past the post the first time he felt that good underneath me that I knew he'd be hard to beat. We got to the 1000 metre mark and as I cruised alongside Stathi Katsidis, he said to me 'Geez you're travelling well' and he wasn't kidding. I knew I had them beaten that far out. The acceleration he showed in the straight was amazing. He's just kept improving every run this horse and the owners and the trainer stayed very loyal to me for doing all the country riding on him, by putting me on at Caloundra.

Few people realise the rigours of being a professional jockey: the constant battle with gaining and losing weight and the ever-present risk involved with what is one of the most dangerous sports in the world. Success in racing requires not only incredible commitment, but also courage and faith in one's own ability.

'The physical side of it does take a toll on the body,' Lyall admits. 'But I've been pretty lucky all my life. I've been a natural at it and I thank my culture for that, because I got them Murri legs!'

Lyall has broken both his ankles and his wrist, and last year he had a bad fall and broke his arm.

'They're things that, as a jockey, you've got in the back of your mind,' he said. 'But you know your own ability – it doesn't really worry me.'

Today, life is good for 54 kilo Lyall who, with wife Michelle and their three children — two daughters and a son — lives in the Brisbane bayside suburb of Redcliffe. 'At the moment I'm Redcliffe's leading jockey, as there are no other jockeys living in the suburb,' quipped Lyall.

Lyall has expressed his wish that his son, Beau-dene, will follow in his footsteps and become a jockey:

> I believe jockeys have a special gene. You have to be light and agile. I'll be happy and very proud if my son becomes a jockey, as he's a natural rider. My brother-in-law has an ex-racehorse up at Tewantin and we put a pad on him and put Beau-dene on top and he's just a natural.

Asked about his long-term aspirations, Lyall said:

> I've ridden successfully as a young rider and I've made my name. There comes a time in your life when you have to take a step back and let the younger people come through and there are a lot of successful younger people coming through. I'm just happy going to the bush and making a living and if I'm in good health when I'm 50, I'll be very proud of what I've achieved in the industry.

In 2012, after not riding for 12 months, Lyall Appo won on Susashi at Eagle Farm in Brisbane for trainer Steele Ryan. Showing 'why he was once regarded as one of the states best country jockeys'. Appo piloted Susashi to an easy two lengths victory. These days Lyall Appo works fulltime as a postman and had not ridden in a race after fracturing his vertebrae in a fall at Narango in southeast Queensland in 2011. Lyall reflected 'I lost interest there for a while during my recovery but my son Beau, is apprenticed to Michael Lakey and he's proven to be a great motivator to get back to riding'.

BRADLEY APPO

Lyall Appo's younger brother, Bradley, followed him into a racing career. His early life mirrored that of his brother. He was taken from his family on three occasions and fostered out. As a result, even to this day he has not met a lot of his relatives. Brad reflected respect and admiration for his brother:

> Lyall started it off first when he started riding. I used to have a horse called Speedy with my foster father. Me and Lyall were pretty close and I used to follow him around like a little lost puppy. Anyway he got me into riding and then Lyall went away to start his apprenticeship and I said to [my] foster father, I'd like to do it too, have a crack at it. That is when I started.

An uncle introduced him to a trainer and he had his first ride in 1982. He loved racing, and loved the horses. Initially he got into quarter-horse racing. It was just 400 metre racing, down the straight, and it was really quick. He stayed with the quarter-horses for about four years before moving to Toowoomba and thoroughbred racing. It took some adjustment, and he had to change his style of riding. He had not ridden thoroughbreds much before but quickly realised that there was much more timing involved than with speed racing. He was able to fall back on his brother for advice.

Brad was another rider who had to stand under the large shadow cast by Darby McCarthy, and it was no easy call following either Darby or his brother.

'Everyone said you are not as good as Darby McCarthy or you're not as good as your brother. But you just have to ride to what you can do. You don't go out and ride like your brother or Darby McCarthy,' Brad said.

Racism is present in racing as in all areas of Australian life and Brad has learnt to deal with it. As an example, at one point a young trainer constantly harassed Brad. He went to the stewards for assistance without gaining any satisfaction. So he took it further and made sure the trainer was very aware that he was in the wrong. But racing is no easy life:

> In racing you have to take a lot of shit, and I have had a lot of bad falls lost a few good mates as well. Racing is not an easy road and it is a tough road but if you get the breaks you are laughing all the way and any young fella who thinks it is going to be easy then they are going to be in for a rude shock. If they had ability I would guide them and give them the encouragement to take it on. There are an awful lot of young Aboriginal boys out there that can ride and have got the ability to ride.

Bradley has seen his fair share of triumphs and setbacks. He has focused his attention on his two children and their sporting abilities:

> Being in at out of foster homes all my life, I want to give my children the best life and show them that they are lucky to have the life they do. We can make it; you can be anything you want to be if you just believe in yourself.

The biggest achievement in his life was breaking into a professional industry that is usually classed as elite:

> I used to look up to my eldest brother [Lyall] who also was a jockey, and my foster father who was a saddle bronc [rider]. He had his own business ring barking, and I wanted to follow in his footsteps.

A fall in 1999, after which the doctors told Bradley he would never ride a horse again, shattered his dreams. Playing it safe, he decided to get a job in which he could help children, as a child protection adviser for Goolburri:

> My job entitles me to give the case workers cultural awareness about Indigenous people and explain to the parents why the department is there. I know how these kids are feeling, and I can relate to a lot of the issues that they have. I'm a proud Aboriginal man because our heritage has been handed down through generations and it makes us who we are today — a loud and proud Aboriginal. I tell the kids something I really believe in: 'Never give up.'

PAUL TIMBERY

Paul Timbery is a La Perouse (Sydney) boy who was apprenticed at the headquarters of racing, Randwick. Paul has won a premiership, ridden a winner on every provincial and metropolitan track in New South Wales, ridden for Gai Waterhouse and won trebles and doubles. In the 1980s, he featured in the book *Barriers for Courses* and was recognised as having the best place strike rate at Canterbury racecourse.

He has just made a comeback from some seven years off after a race fall. The Timbery family is very well known at La Perouse, having witnessed Cook's arrival. Family members are very involved in the Aboriginal community, recognising the importance of Aboriginal education and culture.

The Timberys operate an Aboriginal arts and crafts business, promoting Aboriginal crafts. Paul Timbery's wife, Tracy, is a successful horse trainer who has trained many winners in the country and provincial areas. Their racing colours have been the colours of the Aboriginal flag: red, black and yellow.

ROSALYN AND ROD BYNDER

Rosalyn Bynder, the first (official) female Aboriginal jockey in Western Australia, is steeped in racing bloodlines. As the daughter of late Ascot racing identity and trainer Rod Bynder and granddaughter of retired horse trainer Ken Bynder, Rosalyn says she was born with racing in her blood.

Binder rode in the Broome turf club's first-ever ladies' invitational race, a novel event featuring top female jockeys from all over the country.

'I started riding track work at Ascot when I was 12 or 13, and I rode in my first amateur race when I was 17,' Rosalyn said. Tragedy struck when she was still an apprentice: her 48-year-old father Rod suffered a shock fatal heart attack when he was riding a horse at Ascot in October 2008.

Bynder, then an apprentice jockey, was devastated by the loss of her father. She fell pregnant soon after the tragedy, and took an extended break. However, when her daughter was nine months old, she decided to get back on the horse — literally.

'I wanted to finish my apprenticeship and become a jockey, and now I'm fully fledged,' she said. 'I just want to ride as many winners as I can on the north-west country circuit — from Carnarvon and Roebourne to Port Hedland, Newman and Broome.'

Rosalyn said she also hoped to inspire other young Aboriginal women to enter the industry, and to be a positive role model to her daughter, Charlie. Bynder's grandmother, Dot Bynder, said her son would be very proud of how far his daughter had come.

'We're all very proud of her — deep down we always knew she would finish her apprenticeship off,' she said. 'She wanted to because of her dad.'

Rod Bynder had created history when he had trained bold front-running mare Belle Bizarre to take out the Group 1 Railway Stakes in Perth in 2006. Belle Bizarre led all the way, and held on for victory by a short half-head in the $760,000 Grade 1 Railway Stakes (1600 metres) at Ascot in Perth. In achieving this success as a trainer, Rod Bynder became the first Aboriginal to train a Group 1 winner in Australia by winning the prestigious feature event.

At the time, any immediate recognition of Bynder's breakthrough was thwarted by the post-race collapse of his own father, Ken, who had a heart attack as he left the Ascot racetrack grandstand to celebrate with his son. The hobby trainer later recovered, but Rod was understandably drained after a week of intense emotion. In a hectic period, Bynder surprisingly collected a car as a bonus for winning the Railway; on the flipside, he had watched Rosalyn break a collarbone in a race fall nine days previously. Bynder said at the time:

A SMILING ROS BYNDER CLEARLY LOVES RIDING AND HORSES. PHOTOGRAPH BY LEON MEAD.

> It has just made the week so bizarre. I feel so flat. It has just drained the energy right out of me. I don't know of any Aboriginal trainers, although I think there are a few around, but you don't see them there at Group I races, or even hear about them at Group I races. [But] I was always wondering if in Brisbane or Tasmania, or somewhere like that, which you don't hear about, someone else had done it, but I don't think so. You'd think someone would have written about it otherwise.

Aside from the historical significance, Bynder's training feat was remarkable.

The former jockey was a battler who beat the best in Australian racing with his underrated horse born from a mare that cost the winning owners $1200. Despite Belle Bizarre's effort, it does not rank as Bynder's greatest achievement. He rates bringing up his two daughters — Rosalyn and Aleesha, who worked for Fred Kersley, the trainer of former star Northerly— after their mother left him as the toughest, but most rewarding, thing he has done:

> They were only eight and 10, so I had to bring them up on my own, and they became stablehands at 10 years old. They were stablehands in the morning, would go to school and fall asleep at school, then come home and do the work. That's just how it had to be. We had 25 horses and I didn't know what else to do. [It was] pretty hard on them, but they've grown up pretty well. Getting back to your role models, they've turned out all right, and it works, I'm just so sure of that.

Bynder began his career in racing as a 13-year-old. He rode about 40 winners, including cup winners in the southern Western Australian towns of Albany and Mount Barker. He believes he could have done better:

> I could have (made money) but I wasn't dedicated enough, I was riding races, playing footy, drinking, just no hope, no hope, not dedicated enough. I won a reserves best and fairest for footy while riding — that was in the whole competition — and I weighed just 45 kilos. It was just a joke.

But he matured during a stint interstate breaking in horses for renowned Sydney trainer Neville Begg, and established a reputation for being a hard worker who had a natural knack for taming barrier rogues, the horses he branded 'ferals'. Dedication and bravery marked Rod Bynder: he only employed female stablehands because he believed 'they treat the horses better than the boys'. He was quickly back in the saddle trying to tame a horse just two days after it had dumped him in a fall that crushed his sternum, and the vertebrae in his neck and back:

> I had to ride this wild thing because there was no way I would want the girls on such a dangerous horse. That was the only time it really hurt me. I used to get half-way round and have tears in my eyes, I was that sore. I found out a lot about myself doing that.

Rod Bynder took great pride in his daughter Rosalyn's choice of career. He backed her to the hilt when Western Australian stewards outed senior jockey Pat Carbery for two months on racial grounds. The rider had made derogatory remarks in races to Rosalyn, then an emerging apprentice out west.

'These things are pretty hard on families,' Rod Bynder said. 'You don't like to see kids go through things like that; it was an issue that had to be addressed. You fix it up and get on with things.' He added: 'She has had 100 rides and ridden 16 winners. She's a pretty handy rider, a very good horsewoman. As you can imagine, she has been riding her whole life.

Rod was equally proud of his other daughter: 'Aleesha is one of [trainer] Fred Kersley's main trackwork riders. She can run a stable if I have to go away, she is a very competent girl.'

In 2008, the Perth racing industry was shocked when Rod Bynder tragically passed away. The popular Bynder was loved for his knockabout attitude to life, typified by his 'never say die' attitude. He was only two months shy of his 50th birthday when a massive heart attack robbed him of his life as he worked a horse at early morning trackwork.

He was busy doing what he had always done: educating racehorses in his role as the state's most respected horse breaker. But he was also an accomplished trainer of racehorses in a career highlighted by his Group 1 win with Belle Bizarre in the 2006 Railway Stakes (discussed above). Belle Bizarre was typical of the Bynder stable's horses. A well-known rogue, she took 10 starts to win her maiden at Northam, but once she understood what racing was all about, she developed into a special racehorse.

George Daly knew Bynder well, becoming the master of his apprentice daughter Ros:

> Rod was an extremely popular person. He was admired as a horseman and a single parent. He was fearless with the horses, and could handle any wild beast. It was his perseverance that saw Belle Bizarre develop into a Group 1 winner.
>
> I coached him in football and he was a tenacious, gifted sportsman, who could turn his hand to any sport and excel. He was a workaholic who was still riding the wild ones at an age when the younger blokes would be expected to take over.
>
> Rod will be sorely missed in the industry, because horse men like him do not come along very often. Not only will his skills be missed but his affable nature at trackwork every morning will be impossible to replace. It wouldn't matter how bad you were going, a simple hello from Rod and a look at his cheeky smile would get you moving in the morning.
>
> If it wasn't for Rod, I doubt if Jacks or Better would have even got into the Railway Stakes, let alone won it. He helped me out every morning with a lead pony and we were able to re-educate him.
>
> Rod has left an indelible mark on the industry. His [work] for Indigenous people and his efforts as a single father were probably his greatest achievements.

At Ascot on the Saturday following the funeral, jockeys wore a black armband as a sign of respect for the Rod Binder.

In 2012, Ros Bynder said she was delighted and honoured to be named runner-up in Miss NAIDOC 2012. Bynder was one of 11 entries from a diverse range of backgrounds that depicted a positive and contemporary image of Aboriginal and Torres Strait women in Perth.

> I'm so excited and I can't begin to explain what it feels like,' she said. 'It was an honour to be part of the competition and I had so much fun. It was an unbelievable experience and I'm looking forward to the next few months and assisting and supporting [winner] Rachel [Visser].'

Roslyn Binder continues to carry the courage and determination of her father on to the racetrack in Western Australia.

GAYNOR CHAMBERS

Gaynor Chambers comes from a family steeped in racing tradition. Her three older sisters Carlene Wehr, Ramona Wehr, Leonie (Lulu) Wehr were all jockeys. They were well known for making history and being entered into the *Guinness Book of Records* for almost triple dead heating at Pioneer Park, Alice Springs in a five horse race in 1982. At the time Gaynor was 14 and was only riding track work, but her sisters were certainly an inspiration to follow. Gaynor started riding in 1985 and rode successfully for 17 years only taking breaks inbetween to have two children. During her career Lulu was the only sister she had the opportunity of riding against. They were very competitive on the track but close sisters off it.

At one point after a serious fall and protracted convalescence in hospital, she seriously considered giving the game away. But reading a book about Australia's greatest horse, Phar Lap, gave her the courage and zest to return to the track.

Her perseverance and determination in the tough and uncompromising world of thoroughbred horse racing paid off, and she recorded the enviable record of 26 winners from 100 rides.

Gaynor gives due recognition to her mother, Emmie Wehr, who is recorded as Australia's first Aboriginal female trainer. 'I became apprenticed to mum,' she says. 'And between us, we get the best out of our horses and each other.'

Gaynor grew up on a station 300 kilometres south-east of Alice Springs, and she learned to ride at an early age, breaking in 'reckless bush brumbies that were often as reckless and wild as the wind'. 'I could never turn my back on that feeling of being on a horse,' she says. 'They are my best friends.'

Her love of the Red Centre, 'with its untamed heart', restricts the direction of her career in the future.

'The money and the great tracks are down south,' she says. 'But just at the moment, I'm not ready to leave here.' However she quipped: 'It'd be nice to bring home a winner at Flemington!' (*Australasian Post*, 21 December 1991)

Gaynor's mum Emmie is a trainer still today at Pioneer Park at age 76. Her dad (deceased 1994) was a jockey, there were eight girls in the family, six rode horses, four of those riders were jockeys and Gaynor was the last one to carry the banner for their mother retiring in 2002. Gaynor was the clerk of the course at Alice Springs and competes in various disciplines successfully with two palomino geldings and she also breeds her own performance horses.

My sisters don't have anything to do with racing now, having raised kids and concentrated on other aspects of their lives. It will always remain a part of the history of Alice Springs that an uneducated but very talented horse woman of Aboriginal origin, Emmie Wehr, had four female jockeys that were a huge part of the racing industry in Central Australia.

BIBLIOGRAPHY

Ahern, W 1982, *A century of winners*, Boolarong, Brisbane.
Allan, I 1974, Article in *Turf Monthly*, April.
Arnold, T 1969, Article in *Racetrack*, December.
Arnold, T 2002 'In the sport of kings, prejudice rarely rode', *The Weekend Australian*, 23–24 November.
Baldwin, S 1988, *200 Unsung heroes and heroines of Australia*, Greenhouse, Melbourne.
Bartle, J 1992, Article in *Turf Monthly*, May.
Bernstein, DL 1969, *The first Tuesday in November*, Heinemann, Melbourne.
Brassel, S 1990, *A portrait of racing: horseracing in Australia and New Zealand since 1970*, Simon & Schuster, Sydney.
Britt, E 1974, 'Tricks of the track', in D Ballantine (ed.), *The Australasian book of thoroughbred racing*, Stockwell Press, Melbourne.
Brockman, J 1987, *He rode alone … being the adventures of pioneers Julius Brockman*, Artlook Books, Perth.
Broome, R 1980, *Aboriginal Australians*, Allen & Unwin, Sydney.
Broome, R 1995, 'Victoria', in A McGrath (ed.), *Contested ground*, Allen & Unwin, Sydney.
Cavanough, M 1976, *The Caulfield Cup*, Macarthur Press, Sydney.
Cavanough, M 1983, *The Melbourne Cup 1861–1982*, Lloyd O'Neil, Melbourne.
Clouten, KH 1967, *Reid's Mistake*, Griffin Press, Adelaide.
Clarke, G 1983, Article in *Racetrack*, September.
Clarke B (as told to Camilla Chance) 2003, *Wisdom man*, Viking, Melbourne.
Clendinnen, I 1999, *True stories*, ABC Books, Sydney.
Connelly, R 1974, Article in *Racetrack*, January.
Connors, D 1982, Article in *Racetrack*, November.
D'Arcy, G 1950, *Racing in France*, Societe Industrielle d'Imprimerie, Paris.
Dawson, G 1990, Article in *Turf Monthly*, October.
Dodd, M 2000 *They liked me, the horses, straightaway*, Ginninderra Press, Canberra.
Elder, B 1998, *Blood on the wattle*, New Holland Press, Sydney.
Gadfly Media 1996, *Legends of the racetrack,* Federal Publishing Company, Sydney.
Groome, H 1995, *Working purposefully with Aboriginal students*, Social Science Press, Sydney.
Goodall, H 1996, *Invasion to embassy*, Allen & Unwin, Sydney.
Goodwin, K 1953, *Sports novels*, n.p., Sydney.
Gorman, S 2011, *Legends: The AFL Indigenous Team of the Century 1905–2005*, Aboriginal Studies Press, Canberra.
Grenfell-Price, A 1944, *The comparative management of native peoples in America, New Zealand and Australia*, Royal Australian Historical Society Journal and Proceedings, vol. 30.
Gunson, N 1974, *Australian reminiscences and papers of LE Threlkeld*, AIAS, Canberra.
Hansen Fels, M 1988, *Good men and true*, Melbourne University Press, Melbourne.
Harris, B 1989, *The proud champions,* Little Hills Press, Sydney.
Hasluck, P 1988, *Shades of darkness: Aboriginal affairs 1925–1965*, Melbourne University Press, Melbourne.
Hickie, D 1986, *Gentlemen of the Australian turf*, Angus & Robertson, Sydney.
Horner, J 1994, *Bill Ferguson: fighter for Aboriginal freedom*, Jack Horner, Canberra.
Howe, R 1983, Article in *Turf Monthly*, February.
Hoysted, D 1999, Article in *Turf Monthly*, February.
Kennedy, R 1977, Article in *Racetrack*, June.
Kerwin, D 2010, 'Aboriginal heroes: episodes in the colonial landscape', *Queensland Historical Atlas*, http://www.qhatlas.com.au/content/aboriginal-heroes-episodes-colonial-landscape.

Krygier, M 1997, *Between fear and hope*, ABC Books, Sydney.
Lemon, A 1990, *The history of Australian thoroughbred racing*, Southbank Communications Group, Melbourne.
Lemon, A 2011, 'Storming the barricades: The family history revolution', The Don Grant Lecture, State Library of Victoria, 1 August.
Lewis, D 1997, *A shared history: Aborigines and white Australians in the Victoria River District Northern Territory*, Timber Creek Community Government Council, Darwin.
Maynard, J 1997, 'Fred Maynard and the Australian Aboriginal Progressive Association (AAPA): one god, one aim, one destiny', *Aboriginal History*, vol. 27, pp. 1–13.
McCourt, J 1980, Article in *Racetrack*, December.
McGrath, A. 1987, *'Born in the cattle': Aborigines in cattle country*, Allen & Unwin, Sydney.
JM Miller, J 1985, *Koori will to win,* Angus & Robertson, Sydney.
Miller, M 1985, *Report of the Committee of Review, into Aboriginal Employment and Training Programs*, Government Paper, Canberra.
National Inquiry into the Separation of Aboriginal and Torres Strait Islander Children from Their Families (1997), *Bringing Them Home: Report of the National Inquiry into the Separation of Aboriginal and Torres Strait Islander Children from Their Families*, Commonwealth of Australia, Canberra, http://www.humanrights.gov.au/sites/default/files/content/pdf/social_justice/bringing_them_home_report.pdf.
Owen, P 1984, Article in *Racetrack*, June.
Penton, N 1987, *A racing heart: the story of the Australian turf*, William Collins, Sydney.
Perkins, C 1999, Article in *Koori Mail*, n.d.
Pollard, J 1981, *The Pictorial History of the Australian Turf*, Lansdowne Press, Sydney.
Pollard, J 1988, *Australian horse racing*, Angus & Robertson, Sydney.
Price, AG 1944, The comparative management of native peoples in America, New Zealand and Australia, *The Royal Australian Historical Society Journal and Proceedings*, vol. 30, p. 297.
Ramsland, J and St Leon, M 1993, *Children of the circus*, Butterfly Press, Sydney.
Read, P 1996, *The stolen generations: the removal of Aboriginal children in NSW 1883 to 1969*, NSW Department of Aboriginal Affairs, Sydney.
Reynolds, H 1982, *The other side of the frontier*, Penguin, Ringwood.
Reynolds, H 1990, *With the white people*, Penguin, Ringwood.
Reynolds, H 1994, 'The Aboriginal response', in S Coupe (ed.), *Frontier country*, Weldon Russell, Sydney.
Stevens, F. 1974, *Aborigines in the Northern Territory cattle industry,* ANU Press, Canberra.
Tatz, C 1987, *Aborigines in sport*, Australian society for sports history, Bedford Park, SA.
Tatz, C 1995, *Obstacle race: Aborigines in sport*, UNSW Press, Sydney.
Tatz, C 1996, *Black diamonds*, Allen & Unwin, Sydney.
Wahlquist, A 1998, 'Lie of the land', *The Australian*, 28–29 March.
Weate, W 1966, Article in *Racetrack*, June.
Williams, G St John and Hyland FPM 1980, *The Irish Derby 1866–1979*, JA Allan & Co, London.
Windmill, R 1989, *Geelong racing*, Brown Prior Anderson, Melbourne.
Yarwood, A and Knowling, T 1982, *Race relations in Australia*, Methuen, Sydney.
You'll, K 1955, *History of the South Australian Jockey Club*, Griffin Press, Adelaide.
Young, M, Mundy E and Mundy, D 2000, *The Aboriginal People of the Monaro*, NSW National Parks and Wildlife, Sydney.

Newspapers and periodicals

Adelaide Chronicle, 14 September 1933
Australasian, 29 April 1876; 3 July 1880; 6 November 1880
Australasian Turf Register, 1880–81

Australasian Post, 21 December 1991
Australasian Sketcher, 25 November 1876
Barrier Miner, 12 August 1895
Border Watch, 14 March 1896
Brisbane Courier, 9 November 1882; 22 December 1894
Central Queensland Herald, 5 May 1932
Charleville Times, 7 November 1947
Courier-Mail, 13 August 1999
Daily Guardian, 18, 19 November 1927
Daily Mirror, 15 May 1989
Geelong Advertiser, 11 November 1876; 26 February 1881; 27 April 1882; 26 July 1898; 10 January 1899
Gippsland Times, 25 March 1918
Hamilton Spectator, 6 August 1861
Illustrated Australian News, 7 November 1891
Koori Mail, 21 October 1999
Melbourne Argus, 16 November 1876
Namoi Valley Independent, 18 January 1986
Northern Daily Leader, 25 September 1972
Otago Witness, 26 November 1881
Perth Gazette, 19 April 1834; 6 June 1834; 30 March 1877
Racetrack, May 1983
South Australian Advertiser, 22 June 1882
South Australian Victuallers Gazette, 24 June 1882
Sporting Life, December 1948
Sunday Herald, 8 February 1953
Sunday Mail (Brisbane), 1 September 1935
Sunday Telegraph, 8 February 1953
Sydney Morning Herald, January 1904; 20 May 1922; 1 November 2004
Sydney Sportsman, 6 March 1907
Townsville Bulletin, 10 February 1913
Truth, 6 January 1907
Voice of the North, 12 June 1925
Warwick Examiner and Times, 3 June 1914
WA Times, 25 February 1870; 30 March 1877
West Australian, 28 October 1903
Western Mail, 19 April 1934

INDEX

Aboriginal Education Advancement Society, 99
Aboriginal identity in racing, 13–14, 18–22, 97
Aboriginal protest movements; 1920s, 27; 1930s, 27; 1960s, 27, 96
Aboriginal Tent Embassy, 27
Aboriginal women in racing, 24–5
Aborigines Protection Board, 22
AFL; Aboriginal involvement in, 3
Angles, Cyril, 61
Appo, Beau, 139
Appo, Bradley, 132, 133, 140–1; child protection officer, 141; fall, 141
Appo, Courtney, 102
Appo, Lyall, 132–9; Aboriginality, 136; apprenticeship, 134–5; boxing career, 136–7; comeback, 138; early years, 132–4; first winners, 134; postman, 139; removal from family, 134; retirement from racing, 137–8
Appo, Michelle, 139
apprentice jockeys; conditions faced by, 67–8, 88, 126, 129, 134–5
Arrold, Tony, 95
Aspinall, Mick, 134
Awabakal Co-op, 127

Bardon, James, 117
Barnes, Billy, 108
Barnes, Mal, 101
Barnett, Mick, 124
Bates, Daisy, 67–8
Begg, Neville, 132, 144
Bernstein, David Lee, 42, 44–5
betting; TAB, 4; *see also* bookmakers
'black velvet', 24; *see also* Aboriginal women in racing; pastoral industry
Blackboys' races, 13–14
Boland, George, 128
bookmakers, 16
Booth, Geoff, 129–30; riding school for Aboriginal boys, 130
Bowden, Annie, 48
Bowden, Catherine, 47
Bowden, Michael Sr, 39, 45–6, 47
boxing; popularity of, 2, 136; jockeys in, 116, 129, 136–7; *see also* Lionel Rose
Bradman, Don, 2
Brassel, Tom, 99
Breasly, Scobie, 79
Broderick, Kenny, 116–17; boxing career, 116; discrimination, 116
Brody, Ron, 121
Burnett, Peter, 127

Bynder, Aleesha, 143, 144
Bynder, Dot, 142
Bynder, Rod, 142–5; death, 142, 144; early years, 144; funeral, 145
Bynder, Rosalyn, 142–5; Miss NAIDOC 2012 runner-up, 145

Cadell, Johnny, 1
Cain, John, 100
Cameron, Bruce, 134
Carbery, Pat, 144
Caroona Mission, 124
Casey, Bill, 60
Cassidy, Jim, 135
Cavanagh, Jack, 112
Chambers, Gaynor, 146
Charley, Bob, 79
Clarke, Uncle Banjo, 18
Collins, Norm, 124, 125, 126
Connelly, Eric, 61
Conquest, Pompey, 116
Cook, Billy, 79
Cook, Graham, 136
Cook, Peter, 135
Cox, Mr, 21
Coyle, Jason, 104
cricket; Bodyline series, 2
Croker, Samuel, 110
Cronulla race riots, 20
Curtain, Pat, 82–5
Cushion, George, 112

Daly, George, 145
Daniels, Keith, 76
Darby McCarthy Aboriginal Employment and Training Program, 4, 103–4
Darcy, Les, 75
Date, Mr, 76
Davidson, Harold, 122
Davidson, Stan, 68
Day, Maxie, 91
de Mestre, Etienne, 34
Deebing Creek Aboriginal Home, 21–2
Department of Aboriginal Affairs, 101
Dewsbury, Norman, 70
Dexter, Nancy, 42, 45
Dillon, Sir John, 100
Dittman, Mick, 135
Dixon, Clive, 132
Dodd, Marty, 13
Doncaster, 32
Dries, Doug, 18
Dries, Jimmy, 18, 112–13; as trainer, 113

Dries, John, 123
Duval, Frank, 117, 119; overseas career, 119; as trainer, 119
Duval, Jack, 117–19
overseas career, 119

Easton, Charlie, 94–5
Edwards, Warren, 91
Ellwood, Ros, 132

Fahler, Cliff, 100
Fannie Bay Gaol, 110
Ferry, Sid, 40
Flannigan, Charlie, 110
Flemington Racecourse, 35
see also Melbourne Cup
football, 3; *see also* AFL; Rugby League
Foyster, Lloyd, 101
Freedom Rides, 27, 96
Freeman, Cathy, 28
Frost, Doug, 89

Giretti, Mario, 83
Goodes, Adam, 5, 20, 27
Goodwin, Barbara, 107, 108
Goodwin, Jemimah, 108
Goodwin, Leigh-Anne, 105–8; birth of son, 106; career winners, 107; fatal accident, 105, 108; funeral, 108; hairdressing course, 106; marriage breakdown, 106; racing background, 105
Goodwin, Mark, 105, 107, 108
Goolagong, Evonne, 27, 135
Gorman, Sean, 3
Graham, Paul, 71–4
Great Depression, 2
Guinness Book of Records, 123, 146

Hagan, Barry, 117
Hales, Tom, 32, 38
Harris, Noel, 85
Harris, Wayne, 69
Hart, Reg 'Punter', 127–8
Hatton, Elizabeth McKenzie, 22
Hayden, Alec, 1
Hayes, Denise, 111–12
Heynes, Mick, 61
Herbert, Xavier, 24
Higgins, Roy, 99, 135
Hill, Tommy, 75–6
Hodge, Glen, 123
Hodgson, Doug, 119–21
appearance in *The Sundowners*, 121; apprenticeship, 121; early

INDEX

years, 119–120; head judge at Port Augusta Trotting Club, 121; winning the card, 121
Hodgson, Ian, 121
Hodgson, Jayde, 121
Hodgson, Shirley, 121
Hood, Fred, 123
horses, *see* racehorses
Hutchins, Ray, 82, 84, 85
Hyde, Nola, 40–1

Inglis, Greg, 4–5, 20, 27
James, Roy, 68
jockeys; challenges of making a living, 2–3; physical challenges, 139; weight, 3, 139; *see also* apprentice jockeys
Johnson, Darryl, 115–16
Johnson, Dick, 115
Johnson, Lin, 115
Johnson, Phillip, 115–16
Johnson, Stan, 87, 115–16, 129
Johnson, Wayne, 115–16
Johnston, Malcolm, 135
Johnstone, Rae 'Togo', 61, 62, 112 refusal of British licence, 63
Judge, Les, 87

Kelly, Skeeter, 73
Kennedy, Percy, 111–12
Kersley, Fred, 143
Khan, Prince Aly, 2, 98

Lakey, Michael, 139
Lee, George, 33
Lemon, Andrew, 41–8; Don Grant Lecture, 41
Leslie, Jimmy, 62, 123
Lewis, Danny, 69
Lim, WS, 76–7; death, 77
Lord, William, 60, 129, 136; boxing career, 129; weight problems, 129

Macdonald, Leon, 121
Malcolm, Jeff, 137
Maple Brown, AJ, 71
Marion, Merv, 108, 127
Mathews, David, 124–7 apprenticeship, 124–6; as blacksmith, 127; weight problems, 126–7; youth services work, 127
Mathews, Wendy, 127
Matthews, Darcy, 104
Maynard, Fred, 65–6; death, 66
Maynard, Judy, 76–7, 122; as trainer, 77–9
Maynard, Merv, 60, 64–79, 87, 116, 119, 122, 136; AJC Derby incident, 75–6; apprenticeship, 66–8; country cup circuit, 74–5; death of Alinga, 74; early successes, 69; early years, 65–6; first win, 67; in Asia, 76–7; induction into Aboriginal Sports Hall of Fame, 79; injury, 78; meeting with Queen Elizabeth II, 65, 78–9; New Zealand, 75; offer to move to Asia, 71; return to Australia, 77; thoroughbred bloodstock agency, 77
McCarthy, Darby, 28, 62, 84, 94–104, 105, 106, 130, 135, 136, 140 alcoholism, 100; Australian Democrats candidate, 102; breakdown of marriage, 100; dux of Queensland Turf Club Apprentice School, 97; early years, 94–5; erratic behaviour, 96; final comeback, 102–3; first city winner, 97; lavish lifestyle, 2, 99–100; New Caledonia, 101; overturning of disqualification, 100; pride in Aboriginality, 97, 99; race-fixing charges, 99–100; rehabilitation centre, 101; as role model, 4–5; at Royal Ascot, 98; teaching Aboriginal kids, 101–2; triumphs, 94; weight issues, 101; *see also* Darby McCarthy Aboriginal Employment and Training Program
McCarthy, David, 102
McCarthy, Ted, 'Scobie', 96
McGinley, Mr, 113–14
McGrath, Frank, 119
McHugh, Jim, 40
Melbourne Cup; 1876, 323; 1877, 33–5; 1887, 44; 1952, 69; 1973, 80, 82–5, 86; Darby Munro's wins, 61
Middleton, Eric, 129
Migo, 13
Moore, George, 63, 68, 79, 90, 91–2, 98
Mulley, Athol George, 2, 63, 71, 79
Munro, David Hugh 'Darby', 60–4, 79, 95, 122; family links, 62–3; Jewish background, 60–1; Melbourne Cup wins, 61; refusal of British licence, 63; relationship with punters, 61; support for young Aboriginal riders, 62; suspension, 62; taste for good life, 61–2; as trainer, 62
Munro, Hugh Snr, 61, 62–3
Munro, Jim, 61
Murray, Besley, 113; Calgary Stampede, 114; first win, 114; as horse breaker, 113; Thorpe McConnville's Wild Australia Show, 114
Murray, Freddy, 114

National Inquiry into the Separation of Aboriginal and Torres Strait Islander Children from Their Families, 20–2
O'Brien, Bill, 123–4; bush tucker tours, 124; Hastings Citizen of the Year, 124
O'Sullivan, 'Silent' Leo, 75

Packer, Sir Frank, 70–1
pastoral industry, 1–2; award wages, 2; movement away from, 4; opportunities for Indigenous youngsters, 4; role of Aboriginal women, 24–5
Payten's Paddock, 49, 61
Perkins, Charles, 20, 96
Philips, Harry, 1
Pickwick, Glen, 130–2, 135 accidents, 130–2
Piggott, Lester, 79
Pike, Jim, 112
Plant, Harry, 70
Polson, Mick, 129
Power, Herbert, 33–5
Presnell, Max, 40–1
Protection Acts, 1
Purtell, Jack, 79

Quinton, Ron, 135

racehorses; Alinga, 64, 71–4; Alrello, 99; Alspick, 97; Anna's Pal, 88; Arctic Star, 81; arrival in Australia, 9–10; Belle Bizarre, 142–3, 144; Bernborough, 63; Bicolor, 61; Black Caviar, 4; Blue Era, 75; Bonny Dawn, 114; Briseis, 32–3, 38, 86; Broker's Tip, 98–9; Carew, 119; Cele's Image, 98; Chester, 34; Crewman, 82; Dalray, 69; Darahim, 132; Davey Jones, 68; Denali, 116; Didjeridoo, 91; Divide and Rule, 98–9; Dow Street, 97; Dual Choice, 81; Elton's Son, 138; Empan, 130; Feu d'Artifice, 33; first Indigenous contact with, 9–10; Forest King, 37; Gala Supreme, 82–5, 86; Galleon King, 128; Getelion, 107–8; Glengowan, 84–5; Grey Ghost, 123; Gulf Palm, 71; Hard Lad, 116; Hyperno, 101; Indigenous skill as horsemen, 10; Kerrie Dale, 76; Kingsborough, 32, 33; Kodama, 76; Lord of Persia, 132; Manfred, 61;

INDEX

Melita, 36; Midswain, 97; Minto Crag, 130; Mirror Jack, 78; Miss Ketch, 127; Mullala, 97–8; No Score, 77; Nook, 92; Nyperway, 113; Pantheon, 61; Paragon, 67; Patana, 77; Patient Polly, 98; Peter Pan, 61; Phar Lap, 2, 146; Potter's Field, 112; Prince Razzo, 77; Rakia, 98; Rampion, 61; Regal Problem, 126–7; Revenue, 62–3; Rinkeno, 68; Rio Dell, 134; Rio Sand, 97; Royal Rake, 92–3; Russia, 61; Rusty, 95; Sadie's Son, 90; Salamanca, 69–70; Savanaka, 33–5; Sirius, 61; Southern Speed, 121; Stolen Cash, 127; Summer Fair, 75; Susashi, 139; Tamure, 97; Tauto, 82; Top Level, 71; Tulloch, 124; Vagabond, 62; Wahaweta, 119; Wanton Lass, 88; Warrah King, 68; Willie Win, 88; Yootha, 81; Zephyr Bay, 92
racial barriers, 1
racing; barriers faced by Indigenous riders, 19–20; drop in crowd numbers, 4; drop in number of Indigenous riders, 3–4; as elitist sport, 18; first Indigenous jockeys, 13–14; golden years of, 2; opportunities for Indigenous riders, 2; racism in, 18–22, 61, 89, 114, 116, 122, 140; racism in United Kingdom, 63; *see also* Aboriginal identity in racing
Rankin, Father Peter, 40
Rantall, George, 100
Read, Massa, 112
Reeves, Jimmy, 129
Referendum of 1967, 4
Reys, Frank, 80–6; 1973 Melbourne Cup win, 80, 82–5, 86; accidents, 81, 82; apprenticeship, 81; background, 86; death, 86; early years, 81; move to Melbourne, 81; retirement, 85–6; triumphs, 81
Reys, Noelene, 82
Reys, Shelley, 86
Romano, Azzalin, 70
Rose, Lionel, 27, 135
Rose, Norm, 87–93, 105, 123; fall at Randwick, 92–3; first win, 88; riding as hobby, 91
Rothschild family, 2, 98
Rugby League; Aboriginal involvement in, 3; Indigenous All Stars, 3; Koori Knockout, 3
Ryan, Steele, 139

Sandy, 13–14
Savage, Matt, 24
Schumacher, Mel, 75–6
Sellwood, Neville, 79, 124
Shaw, Run Me, 71
Shaw, Run Run, 71
Shelly, Gordon, 81
Sinclair, Bobby, 97–8
Smeardon, Bob, 99–100
Smith, Ken, 76, 78
Smith, Sir Abel, 97
Smith, TJ, 70, 123
Smith, WA, 92
sport; importance to Indigenous people, 3; prominent Aborigines in, 27; *see also* AFL; boxing; Rugby League
St Albans, Anastasia, 37
St Albans, Peter, 30–48 brother, 46–7; career triumphs, 31; death, 37; first Melbourne Cup win (1876), 32–3, 37, 86; first race (and winner), 31–2; as horse trainer, 37; as Michael Bowden Jnr?, 40–1, 44, 46–7; mystery of origins, 37–48; other Melbourne Cup rides, 36; retirement, 36–7; second Melbourne Cup win (1877), 33–5
St Albans' Stud, 31, 34, 39, 41, 62, 63
Stevens, Charlie, 121
Stolen Generations, 20–2, 24
Stolen Generations inquiry, *see* National Inquiry into the Separation of Aboriginal and Torres Strait Islander Children from Their Families
Strong, Neil, 130–7
Symons, Carl, 136–7

Tatz, Colin, 13
Taylor, Dennis, 123
Taylor, Gordon, 60, 62, 87, 122–3
Thompson, Jack, 77, 79, 126
Thompson, Joe, 33–5, 44
Thompson, Robert, 68, 69
Thompson, Vic, 70, 71
Threkeld, Reverend LE, 9
Thurston, Jonathon, 27
Timbery, Paul, 141
Timbery, Tracy, 141
Tinson, Jimmy, 91, 92, 129
Tinson, Keith, 62, 66, 71, 87–8, 115, 122; death, 91
Tracey, Billy, 90
Trail, Jim, 124
Turnbull, Norman, 97

Victoria Racing Club, 41

Wade, Billy, 129
Wade, John, 69
Waite, Billy, 1
Wall, Roley, 116
Wallace, 'Jackey'/'Jackie', 14–15
Waterhouse, Gai, 25, 141
Wehr, Carlene, 146
Wehr, Emmie, 146
Wehr, Leonie (Lulu), 146
Wehr, Ramona, 146
weight, *see* jockey weight
White, Harry, 135
White, Hon. James, 34
Wiggins, Larry, 75
Wildenstein family, 2
Wildenstein, Daniel, 98
Williams, Neil, 136
Williamson, Bill, 79
Wilson, James Jr, 33, 41
Wilson, James Sr, 31–2, 33–5, 36, 38–9, 46, 62, 63; as Peter St Alban's biological father?, 38–9, 43; *see also* St Albans, Peter
Wilson, Joseph, 39–40
Wilson, William, 33
Windmill, Robert, 38, 40, 42
women in racing, *see* Aboriginal women in racing
Woodhouse, Frederick, 30, 38
Wooten, Frank, 40
Wooten, Stanley, 40
Wootton, Dick, 62

Yakara Station, 94
Yanga Station, 113–15
Yarn'n Aboriginal Employment Services, 103
Yarnteen, 127

Zilber, Maurice, 98